JUMP-START YOUR SUCCESS

23 Top Speakers Share Their Insights for Creating More Success, Wealth and Happiness

FEATURING

James Malinchak
Co-Author, Chicken Soup for the College Soul
"2-Time National College Speaker of the Year"
Founder, www.BigMoneySpeaker.com

& Brian Tracy
Legendary Speaker, Author, Trainer & Consultant
Spoken to Over 5 Million People Worldwide

Warning – Disclaimer
The purpose of this book is to educate and entertain. The author or publisher does not guarantee that anyone following the ideas, tips, suggestions, techniques or strategies will become successful. The author and publisher shall have neither liability or responsibility to anyone with respect to any loss or damage caused, or alleged to be caused, directly or indirectly by the information contained in this book.

Table of Contents

THE NEWEST, FASTEST, EASIEST WAY TO MAKE ADDITIONAL BIG MONEY IN YOUR BUSINESS!

By James Malinchak

James Malinchak has delivered over 2,200 presentations for business groups, corporations, colleges and youth organizations worldwide for audiences ranging from 20 to 12,000 and has done so without being famous, any advanced academic degrees and without any speaker designations from any speaker associations.

He's written 16 books…including co-authoring the BEST-SELLER, Chicken Soup for the College Soul, and he was named Marketer of the Year by Marketing Guru's Dan Kennedy & Bill Glazer.

James owns 6 businesses, has read and researched over 2,500 books on personal and professional development, and has even been interviewed on the Celebrity Red Carpet by Hollywood Interviewer Robin Leach. He also works with numerous celebrities and professional athletes.

James is called **"Big Money Speaker™"** and is called by numerous people **"America's #1 Speaker Trainer for Anyone Who Wants to Make Big Money As a Highly Paid Public Speaker!"**

If you've ever dreamed of making the kind of BIG MONEY that only being a public speaker can bring you, then visit:

www.BigMoneySpeaker.com
www.CollegeSpeakingSuccess.com
www.MillionaireSpeakerSecrets.com

The Newest, Fastest, Easiest Way to Make Additional
BIG MONEY in Your Business!

Have you ever sat in a seminar listening to a speaker and while you were listening you said to yourself, "I bet he/she is making a lot of money talking about what they know!"…or…"I could do that"…or…"I would be so much better than that speaker if I were speaking!"

That's exactly how I began my entire speaking career. I remember sitting in an audience listening to a speaker talking about the most basic topic and wondering how much he was getting paid. After he finished his presentation, I asked if I could take him to lunch, which he kindly agreed. Over lunch, I let him tell me about his topic, as it was obvious he was passionate about it. Finally after 30-minutes into our lunch, I got enough courage to ask, "Could I ask how much you were just paid for delivering that 45-minute presentation?" To my surprise he said, "$10,000!"

What!?! I couldn't believe it! I was SO shocked at the kind of money he was being paid for simply talking about something he knew!

Immediately, I knew I was going to start adding public speaking as a part of my business, even though I had no clue where to start or how to begin! And I can tell you now that looking back, making the decision to add public speaking to my current business was the absolute BEST business decision I ever made. And now, I am on a mission to encourage and train as many business owners as possible to, not change their current business model, but to simply add public speaking as an add-on to their current business.

When you understand the power of adding public speaking to your current business and just how much more BIG money you can add to your bank account weekly, monthly and yearly, you will soon realize that you have been losing out on hundreds of thousands (maybe millions) of dollars…and hopefully, you will join those of us who understand that adding public speaking to your current business (whatever business you are in) can instantly bring you BIG money and a blessed lifestyle.

Let me share with you 6 reasons public speaking should be immediately added as a part of your business model!

Credibility – Would you like instant credibility as a "perceived" authority in your market? Or, if you're already established in your market, would you like to instantly rise to the top as being thought of as THE go-to person for your niche, product and service? Then public speaking can instantly do that for you. When prospects have the chance to sit in a room and listen to you talk about a topic, instantly they assume you must be a leading authority/guru because you are the one speaking on the topic. You receive a level of credibility you cannot get any other way.

Free Publicity – Newspapers, magazines and trade journals love to write free articles about you as they see you as an expert. They also call-on you to give quotes about certain topics for articles they are writing for their readers. Also, you are invited to write guest articles for subscribers.

Paid Checks – For years, I have been one of the leading fee-paid speakers in both the corporate/association market and the college/university market. I know some people don't like getting paid checks for talking about what they know, but I love it! I think it's the coolest thing when I get paid $20,000 for a 45-minute presentation talking about ideas that I would talk about anyway on a daily, weekly, monthly basis. Did I start at $20,000? No. When I really got the business side of speaking cranking and learned who the people are that have the money, I was pulling-in $5,000-$7,500 for a 45-minute talk. Then I quickly went to $10,000…then $15,000…then to $20,000. And here's the cool thing for you. Not only do you get paid a guaranteed check, but you also get to travel to some great resort areas while getting treated in a VIP First-Class way. Gotta love it!

Platform Offering – There are many events where, although you may not be paid a check to speak, you can speak and offer your products to the audience in the form of continuing education so audience members can continue to learn from you after your talk is finished. You could offer continuing learning in the form of books, CDs, DVDs, home study courses, live seminar trainings, teleseminars, group mastermind coaching, one-on-one coaching, consulting, etc. When you deliver a talk filled with information that benefits the audience, many of them will want more of you and your ideas. It's your responsibility to allow audience members to continue learning from you so they can be better. And, you can make an incredible amount of extra money while helping a lot of people. I can't think of anything better in business – getting to talk about something that I enjoy that is helping audience members, while making BIG money.

Spin-Off Business – The spin-off business from public speaking can be amazing. What is spin-off business? Spin-off business is when you receive additional business opportunities from audience members. Imagine, you are giving a talk to a group talking on a topic you enjoy and when you finish, several audience members walk-up to you thanking you for a great talk. Then they ask if you would be able to give that same talk for their group. They can pay you a speaking fee (check) or they may not pay you a check but will allow you to offer your continuing education so their audience members can invest in themselves after your presentation. In addition to getting spin-off business from audience members, you can also get spin-off business from the original person or group who booked you to speak. They can re-book you for their next event or even book you for additional multiple events.

Build Your List & An Immediate Following…FAST! – I love this one! When you speak to a group, you immediately attract a group of raving fans who want to follow you and want to be marketed to by you. Public speaking is one of the best ways to start lead generation and list building because of the immediate connection audience members have with you.

Because you were the person who delivered the talk, audience members form a bond with you and see you as a credible source. They want to receive your emails and direct mail pieces. I still have people on my list buying products and attending my speaker boot camps who heard me speak 10 years ago to an audience.

Adding public speaking as a part of your current business is, by far, the BEST business decision you can make. It is, without a doubt, pound-for-pound, hour-for-hour, the BEST business model and the newest, fastest, easiest way to make additional BIG MONEY in your business! And here's the good news, it's simply a learned skill that you can easily learn.

I have taken numerous business owners who had no clue how to start, where to begin or what they should even talk about, and showed them step-by-step a simple recipe to follow that had them making BIG money in less than 30-days by simply talking about what they know. You can do it – the time is now! All you need to learn is the simple recipe!

THE
FOUNDATION
OF SUCCESS

by: Brian Tracy

Brian Tracy is one of the world's foremost thought leaders on personal and business success. In the last 30 years he's consulted for more than 1,000 companies, including IBM, Ford, Federal Express, and Hewlett Packard, and has spoken to over 5 million people worldwide on the subjects of Sales, Business, Leadership, Self-Esteem, Goals, Strategy, and Success Psychology. He's the top selling author of over 55 books, including *Eat That Frog!*, and has written and produced more than 300 audio and video learning programs, including the worldwide, best-selling *Psychology of Achievement.* He's one of the most sought after success coaches and has transformed the lives of millions. For more information on Brian Tracy programs go to www.briantracy.com.

A young woman once wrote to me and told me that her whole life had taken a different turn since she listened to one of my programs and heard the question, "What one great thing would you dare to dream if you knew you could not fail?"

She wrote that, up to that time, this was a question she had never even dared to consider, but now, she thought of nothing else. She had realized in a great blinding flash of clarity, that the main thing separating her from her hopes and dreams was her belief in her ability to achieve them.

Most of us are like this for most of our lives. There are many things that we want to be, and have and do, but we hold back. We are unsure because we lack the confidence necessary to step out in faith in e direction of our dreams.

Abraham Maslow said that the story of the human race is the story of men and women "selling themselves short." Alfred Adler, the great psychotherapist, said that men and women have a natural tendency toward feelings of inferiority and inadequacy. Because we lack confidence, we don't think we have the ability to do the kind of things that others have done, and in many cases, we don't even try.

Just think! What kind of a difference would it make in your life if you had an absolutely unshakable self-confidence in your ability to achieve anything you really put your mind to? What would you want and wish and hope for? What would you dare to dream if you believed in yourself with such deep conviction that you had no fears of failure whatsoever?

The wonderful thing about these questions is that now we know how you can develop your self-confidence to the point where there is nothing that you won't attempt. It's common for most people to start off with little or no self-confidence, but as a result of their own efforts, they become bold and brace and outgoing. And we've discovered that if you do the same things that other self-confidence men and women do, you too will experience the same feelings and get the same results.

The foundation of self-confidence is to like and accept yourself unconditionally as a valuable and worthwhile human being. There is nothing more important than this. The more you like and respect yourself and consider yourself to be a thoroughly good person, the more you will believe in yourself and the more confidence you will have in your ability to say and do the right things at the right time.

Dr. Nathaniel Branden calls self-esteem, "your reputation with yourself." The better your reputation is with yourself, the more you will like yourself. Put another way, the clearer you are about your values, about what you believe in and stand for, the more you will like yourself and the more likely it is that you will have a deep-down sense of calmness and self-assurance.

The key is to be true to yourself, to be true to the very best that is in you, and to live your life consistent with your highest values and aspirations.

Take some time to think about who you are and what you believe in and what is important to you. Make the decision that you will never compromise your integrity by trying to be or say or feel something that is not true for you. Have the courage to accept yourself as you really are, not as you might be, or as someone else thinks you should be, and that taking everything into consideration, you are a pretty good person.

After all, the odds are more than fifty billion to one that there will ever be another person just like you. Each person is unique. They have their own talents, skills and abilities that make them extraordinary. No one, including yourself, has any idea of your capabilities or of what you might do or become. Perhaps the hardest thing in life is to accept how extraordinary you really are and you really can be, and then to incorporate this awareness into your attitude and personality. Liking and believing in yourself is the foundation of a healthy self-confidence and the starting point of great happiness and success.

Lasting self-confidence really comes from a sense of control. It is when you feel very much in control of yourself and your life that you feel confident enough to do and say the things that are consistent with your highest values. Psychologists today agree that a feeling of being "out of control" is the primary reason for stress and negativity and for feelings of inferiority and low self-confident. And the way for you to get a solid sense of control over every part of your life is for you to set clear goals and objectives. It's for you to establish a sense of direction based on purposeful behavior aimed at pre-determined ends.

Lasting self-confidence arises when you absolutely know that you have the ability to get from where you are to wherever you want to go. You are behind the wheel of your own life. You are the architect of your own destiny and the master of your own fate.

Happiness has been defined as the progressive realization of a worthy ideal. The same holds true for self-confidence. When you set a goal and make a plan, and then work step-by-step toward making your goal a reality, you feel strong and capable and in control of your life. You feel like a winner. Your self-confidence goes up and your willingness to take on even greater challenges and opportunities increases. And the more you accomplish, the more you feel that you are capable of accomplishing.

Instead of being pre-occupied by the fear of failure, and loss, as most people are, you focus on the opportunity and the possible gains of achievement. With clearly defined goals and a track to run on, you become success-oriented and you gradually build your self-confidence up to the state where there is very little your will not take on. And the key is to set your goals and then work progressively toward their attainment.

In conjunction with clear goals, another essential way to build your self-confidence, through positive knowing rather than positive thinking, is to become very good at what you do. The flip side of self-esteem is called "self-efficacy" or the ability to perform effectively in your chosen area.

Whenever you do a job well or complete a task successfully, your self-esteem and self-respect go up. You experience a sense of personal pride that manifests itself in a confidence and willingness to take on even bigger challenges.

You can raise your self-confidence instantly by the simple act of committing yourself to becoming excellent in your chosen field. When you burn your mental bridges behind you and resolve to pay any price, make any sacrifice, or invest any amount of time or money to be the best at what you do, you become a different person. You immediately separate yourself from the average individual who drifts from job to job, and accepts mediocrity as the acceptable standard.

THE ATTRACTION OF SUCCESSFUL LEADERSHIP

by Andrea Adams-Miller

Andrea Adams-Miller, MS, CHES, "The Sexuality Tutor, reveals the secrets to ignite the spark, fire, and passion as "A Leading Authority in Healthy Relationships and Healthy Sexuality." As Executive Director of www.SexualityTutor.com, and www.AndreaAdamsMiller.com, Andrea, a three time author, consistently delivers dynamic content through energetic public speaking and award-winning radio hosting on www.SexTalkLiveRadio.com. As an intimacy and relationship specialist; business consultant; life coach; and motivational speaker, she has been Ohio's "AAUW Young Leader of the Year" and "Business & Professional Women's Young Careerist of the Year." Andrea, contributing author for "What Women Want," "Encyclopedia for Sex and Society," and "Contemporary Sexuality" was interviewed for 20/20, TIME, Prime, and WebMD.

Andrea Adams-Miller

P.O. Box 443

Findlay, OH 45839

419-722-6931

andreaadamsmiller@gmail.com

"If your actions inspire others to dream more, learn more, do more and become more, you are a leader."

~John Quincy Adams

Although attraction is often synonymous with dating or relationships, attraction for the purpose of this article is equivalent to a sense of respect and power to which other people feel drawn. It is this type of attraction that causes others to gravitate towards a particular person as the perceived leader, ultimately resulting in positions of appointed or acquired leadership. With this attraction, colleagues and subordinates assume their individual and group roles placing their trust and confidence in their leader.

Attraction may initiate leadership; however, when it comes to successful leadership there are three main areas of distinction that determine perceived leadership success. These three main areas include leadership traits, leadership behaviors, and leadership styles. Mastering each of these areas equates in the likelihood of being perceived as a successful leader resulting in continued follower attraction.

The traits of successful leadership vary depending on the type of organization, group, or business of which the leader is in charge. Despite variability in the ranking of the successful leadership traits, research reveals overlapping key successful leadership traits include social participation, self-confidence, and assertiveness (Beebe & Masterson, 2009). At the same time, too much of a good thing contributes to attributes of leadership diminishing success or even resulting in failure. Therefore, it is wise for a successful leader to recognize the differences between social participation and social dominance, self-confidence and overconfidence, and assertiveness and aggressiveness.

To expand further, leaders who involve themselves in the community by networking with many people inviting others to discuss their ideas and interests will be revered as friendly and social. However, if the leader dominates the conversations discussing their own projects and accomplishments, they may inadvertently isolate others minimizing successful leadership potential. Likewise, confidence is having the faith to believe in your abilities as a leader, whereas overconfidence is perceived as presumptuous behavior resulting in follower concern that the leader has overstepped their authority evoking distrust. Similarly, an assertive leader presses boundaries in such a way that followers respect the need for expansion or growth. On the flip side, an aggressive leader pushes through boundaries alienating followers and creating hostility. Accordingly, successful leadership can be challenging, yet easy to obtain as follower attraction will continue to flourish as leaders continually develop the leadership traits of social participation, self-confidence, and assertiveness.

Although the acquisitions of leadership traits are an integral part of successful leadership, leadership behaviors are equally important. According to Beebe & Masterson (2009), to maintain follower attraction, a leader must incorporate certain behaviors to help move a group towards their identified goal. Therefore, a leader must initiate ideas to stimulate identification of problems and deliberate solutions before decisions are made prematurely. Along these lines, a successful leader will revisit a motion to allow for elaboration to make sure enough time has been allotted for decisions to be mulled over. With this, a successful leader will recap the previous ideas to make sure a plausible solution was not dismissed prematurely (Beebe & Masterson, 2009). Consequently, a successful leader will gain further follower attraction by practicing these behaviors prior to delegating action. However, the aforementioned leadership behaviors exceed those listed.

Successful leadership requires the ability to keep peace among the constituents. Successful leadership requires inclusive behaviors such as inviting contributions from quiet or absent members. Additionally, successful leadership means attending to the needs of the followers by raising morale of the group by praise, recognition, or acknowledgement (Beebe & Masterson, 2009). However, recognition acceptance is dependent on the recipient's desire. Therefore, learning an individual's desire of public praise or private acknowledgement will help you maintain leadership attraction results Overall, a successful leader acts using behaviors that enhance group processes, thereby increasing follower attraction.

By integrating leadership behaviors into your personal leadership style, a leader is more likely to succeed. However, leadership styles are not equally revered. In group situations, leaders who command respect, dictate orders, and criticize dictating in an authoritative style reflect many of the negative leadership traits previously suggested to avoid (Beebe & Masterson, 2009). Therefore, it should be no surprise when the followers are no longer attracted to the leadership of their commander. Henceforth, the followers are likely to stage a coup instigating an overthrow to put a more attractive leader in their predecessor's position. This is quite discerning for the authoritative leader who often has great passion for his cause and most likely has placed considerable heart and physical labor into the group's project. However, once the group has been isolated from the leader with such a commanding style, the followers are no longer able to see the good intentions of the dictator. Rather, the members turn away. This is most frustrating for all members involved including the overthrown leader resulting in delayed goals and disrupting cohesiveness.

In direct correlation, a leadership style that is too laissez-faire results in disruption if the members need more guidelines or intervention to determine their course of action (Beebe & Masterson, 2009). Although, a laissez-faire leadership style can be positive for an independent group of critical thinkers, this style doesn't create a feeling of attraction towards the leader. Rather, the group often concludes that the leader was unnecessary or slack in their contributions.

Therefore, a more satisfactory style of leadership, which is most likely to lead to success, is a democratic style. However, according to research, leaders utilizing democratic leadership styles are not most attractive even though these leaders bring order, act positively, and generate satisfaction (Beebe & Masterson, 2009). On the flip side, the most attractive successful leaders are those that use a combination of styles to fulfill the needs of their members. Therefore, fluidity in leadership style remains most attractive in response to the situation. This most attractive style is referred to as transformational leadership. Transformational leadership attends to the intellectual, individual, ideational, and inspirational needs of the memberships resulting in shared vision towards goal attainment (Beebe & Masterson, 2009).

With attraction of successful leadership in mind, it is imperative for a leader to portray attractive leadership traits, leadership behaviors, and leadership styles. For a leader to succeed to their highest potential, they need to consider their ability to reflect positive leadership traits including social participation, self-confidence, and assertiveness. Likewise, a successful leader needs to showcase their traits by demonstrating leadership behaviors such as initiating ideas, revisiting previous motions, and summarizing events or discussions. Lastly, a successful leader needs to develop individual style of successful leadership by observing the needs of the groups then adapting authoritative, laissez-faire, and democratic attributes towards a transformational leadership style that meets the particular needs of the group. Although, leadership is challenging, the rewards of leadership reveal themselves through the group accomplishments resulting in a most attractive leader.

Works Cited:

Beebe, Steven A. & Masterson, John T. Communication in Small Groups Principles and Practices. Boston: Pearson Education, Inc. 2009. Print.

SUCCESS AND FITNESS: WHAT'S MY MOTIVATION?

By Rex Causey

Rex Causey is a gifted teacher, coach, personal trainer and speaker on fitness and success. Constantly keeping up with the latest information and newest studies concerning health and fitness, he strives to serve others by sharing with them his knowledge of better fitness habits for a healthier lifestyle. Coach Causey is not just an advocate of a healthy lifestyle for others but also applies the same principles and techniques he teaches to his own everyday fitness routine.

"I don't have time to workout."
"It's too hard to 'eat right'."
"I don't have the money to join a gym or hire a trainer."

If you are reading this chapter, I am willing to bet you have dealt with these thoughts at some point (I know I have and still do!). However, because you are reading this book, I am convinced that you are a person who constantly seeks self improvement no matter what level of success you have gained. My hope, in this chapter, is that you will realize the transforming effect personal fitness can have on your life, and that you will see motivation for better fitness all around you. Be liberated from stress, guilt, fear, and EXCUSES!

Pursuing personal fitness and being motivated in it for life requires a "thought makeover" before anything else. This is evident when one considers that a person cannot solve a dilemma by thinking and living in the same way they were when the dilemma was created. You must understand that how you think determines who you are and how you will act; therefore, in order to positively affect your behavior you want to properly shape your thinking for the better. What mindset should you have on your own fitness then? Think of personal fitness as individual fitness, of course, but NOT as self-centered fitness. In other words, while you, the individual, engage in personal fitness or the lack thereof, your habits (good or bad) impact more than just yourself.

It's time to start thinking about who really matters most when it comes to staying healthy and fit. Is there a bigger reason, a greater motivation than being fit for your own sake? Emphatically, yes! Be personally fit for the sake of your family: for your spouse and your children, for God, for your close friends. If it is only for yourself, then it is in vain and will only lead to a dead-end with more made-up excuses for why you can't achieve better fitness. You must realize that there are reasons, beyond yourself, for which you ought to seek a healthier you. So the next time you feel like you can't workout or that, "eating right," is too hard, just remember that you are not training and eating for one, but for 3...God, family, and friends. Remove yourself from the picture so you can start seeing those around you who are affected by your excuses for not living fit. Then think about how you will benefit them with your choice to be fit for life starting right NOW!

Once the motivation shifts from self-centered to others-centered we can look at how our personal fitness habits impact other areas of our lives such as our careers, playing with our kids, doing recreational activities, or simply walking up the stairs. Knowing the tremendously positive affects that working out and eating right has on the body, it is easy to see how increasing personal fitness will benefit your life in all areas as well as those around you.

The motivation is there now, but where do you start? Below I will share some secrets to revolutionizing your personal fitness without feeling overwhelmed. As you begin to master these points, I encourage you to teach them to others so you can share your fitness success! After all, our focus is others-centered first.

Start a workout journal.

Buy a journal for your workouts. It can be as simple as a spiral bound notebook. Plan and write down your workouts ahead of time. Have your exercises, weight ranges and set/rep ranges ready to go BEFORE you arrive at the gym. Bring your journal with you every time and record your performance in order to track progress.

Weight and cardio training should each be done 2-3 times per week.

Cardio training should be done on non-weight training days and vice versa. Weight training days should involve similar muscle groups being worked. (i.e.: Monday - chest, shoulders, triceps or Wednesday - hamstrings, quads, gluteus, calves)

Spend no more than 45 minutes maximum on cardio or weight training.

You do not have to spend hours in the gym. You could spend as little as 15 minutes in the gym and have an effective workout. It's a matter of being intense, focused, and prepared. Do not chat during your workout time. Do that afterward. STAY FOCUSED AT ALL TIMES.

Quality over quantity: research and study proper form and techniques.

Always put quality of the exercise before quantity of the weights or cardio. Correct form and technique will prevent injury and give you maximum results!

Break records every workout and every week! Always seek to improve.

If you bench pressed 180 lbs. for 3 sets of 12 reps then you need to move up weight to 185 lbs. the next time you bench press. If you ran 2 miles in 15 minutes then your goal is to run it in a lesser time (such as 14:45) the next time you do the 2 mile run. This is extremely rewarding by the end of your 6th week of consistent exercise because you can look back in your journal and remember just how far you have come! If ever you notice a plateau in progress then change up your routine to help break more records.

A simple internet search on the benefits of regular exercise and balanced nutrition can help you find tons more information than I just shared with you, whether it is exercise programs or fitness facts. For instance: facts on how better fitness boosts your energy level, helps manage stress, releases tension, improves sleep patterns making one more rested, increases strength and flexibility, increases self-confidence and self-esteem, counters anxiety and depression, and increases enthusiasm and optimism. Boost that energy by adding some regular exercise to your week and replacing a few sugary foods/drinks with fruits, veggies and water. Notice I did not say you had to replace EVERYTHING sugary. NO WAY! That would drive you insane. Don't try to be perfect, just strive to be better.

No human being on this earth ever has or ever will be perfect. Seeking perfection will only kill motivation. If you want to improve your fitness level and if there is one thing you get from this chapter it should be this: Desire earnestly to be better today than you were yesterday. Seek to be BETTER and remember that it is more than just you that is being impacted by your fitness habits.

THOUGHTS ON SUCCESS

By J.J. Cohen

Having turned $30K into $600K, J.J. Cohen has run his own investment firm for the last 8 years. Previously, he had a 20 year career as an actor -Film credits include BACK TO THE FUTURE 1, 2 and 3, ALMOST FAMOUS, and THE PRINCIPAL. He's worked with top names Steven Spielberg, Robert Zemeckis and Cameron Crowe as well as Kevin Costner, Louis Gossett Jr. and Michael J. Fox. Resuming his film career and traveling extensively throughout the U.S., Europe and Asia, Mr. Cohen enjoys a busy schedule as a Speaker, Author, Investor and Entrepreneur.

Email:jjcrunch@hotmail.com

www.jcohencapital.com

www.spirithreadsintl.com

www.jjcohenspeaks.com

www.jjcoheninternational.com

www.imdb.com/name/nm0169454/

When I was 26 years old, I took a road trip to the Grand Canyon with my then brother–in–law, Mike. In one of the souvenir shops, I found a T-shirt with a picture of a man standing on the edge of the Grand Canyon taking in the vast panoramic view…I remember him looking somewhat small and inconsequential compared to the great Canyon but then on the side of the picture was printed this quote:

> **"…Success is to be measured not so much by the position that one has reached in life as by the obstacles which he has had to overcome while trying to succeed."**
> **– Booker T. Washington**

As I look at my bio on the opposite page, thinking about Mr. Washington's words, I'm reminded that the successes listed only tell half the story. The other half, of course, is the setbacks, obstacles and outright failures that I've had to overcome, both personally and professionally, in order to succeed.

I've discovered through the years that what seemed like "negatives" or apparent failures at the time, were, in fact, extremely crucial in the success that followed. Further, I've found that it's only through being willing to risk failure and then, more importantly, learning from those failures that we grow and master <u>how</u> to be successful.

And what does it mean to risk failure? It means to <u>TRY</u> even when you're not assured of the outcome. Now I know, typically, as "achievers", we don't like to think of the word, "<u>TRY</u>". I once heard a speaker share from the stage, "TRYING IS DYING", he proclaimed. "You don't try to get up out of a chair," he said, "You either do it or don't do it." The audience, myself included, all nodded in agreement. "Yes, there is no trying, ONLY doing", we concluded!

Now this sort of black and white statement is great for a motivational talk however there's one problem - Most of life is a gray area, it's not clear-cut and there are exceptions to most every rule.

To address the Speaker's chair analogy - my mother is 77 years young. She used to be able to just stand right up, as the Speaker referred to, accomplishing this task quite easily. However, a few years ago, she started having problems standing up. So after trying and failing several times to just stand right up, she *tried* leaning on something for leverage to push herself up. That didn't work. Next, she *tried* to pull herself up, holding onto something for balance. That, too, didn't work!! Finally, she *tried* to rock back and forth to gain momentum and this time…SUCCESS!!

From this basic example, you can see how this doesn't just apply to entrepreneurs but rather to anyone who has the courage to push through towards ANY goal despite the obstacles. So don't let the risk of failure, of trying without knowing, stand in the way of your success since trying and failing may be a part of your path to get there. Bottom line - If you don't try, you don't have even a chance at success.

Another obstacle to success is what I refer to as "The War Inside". Simply stated, not letting go of resentments or being able to forgive in a timely manner can make one miserably ineffective for a period of days, months or even years. It can not only hinder one's professional endeavors but can affect one's personal relationships as well.

I was closing down my parent's restaurant when a guy came in the back door, put a gun to my head and DEMANDED money! I was just 19.

When I resisted, still in shock, he hit me over the head with the butt of his gun and drew blood. He told me to get down on the floor, take off my clothes and proceeded to tie my hands behind my back with my shoelaces.

Laying there, humiliated and frightened, I turned to watch him and he kicked me in the face with his work boot!

I don't really remember what happened next but that night marked the end of innocence for me. He didn't just take some money, he took my spirit. The guilt and shame I felt was unbearable and the next day I WOKE UP ANGRY, MAD AT THE WORLD!! I REALLY WANTED TO HURT SOMEBODY!! I HAD THE WORST KIND OF ANGER YOU COULD POSSIBLY HAVE BECAUSE IT'S THE HARDEST TO GET RID OF!! I HAD JUSTIFIED ANGER - I WASN'T JUST "PLAYING THE VICTIM", I WAS THE VICTIM!!

I had no idea how to get through the anger and let it go…And then I heard this story:

> Little boy comes running into his father's office and says, "DADDY, DADDY, can we go play!?!" The father, sitting at his desk, barely looks up and says, "Son, Daddy's busy right now but when Daddy's done, we can go play." So the little boy leaves. Ten minutes later, the little boy comes running back into the room. "DADDY, DADDY, can we go play now?" The father, getting a little agitated says, "Son, Daddy's working right now so go back outside and when Daddy's done, we can play." The little boy leaves the room again and ten minutes later comes running back in and says, "Daddy, Daddy, can we go play and the Father just about loses it, looks around and sees a National Geographic and opens it up to a picture of a map, it's a map of the world and he RIPS the page out and tears it up into a bunch of little pieces and says, "Here son, Daddy made you a puzzle, now go outside and put the puzzle

together and when you're done, we'll go play." As the little boy leaves the room, the father breathes a sigh of relief, thinking, he can now finally get some work done. But five minutes later, the little boy comes back into the room and places the puzzle on the father's desk. The Father looks over and tears come to his eyes. He can't believe what he sees. The puzzle's all put together perfectly. There isn't a piece out of place...He even had time to tape it. The father looks down at his son, and says, "Son, this is beautiful... How'd you do this?" The son looks up at his father and says, "It was easy Daddy – I just turned the pieces over and on the back was a picture of a man...I just put the man together and the world fell into place."

The greatest obstacle we have to success is ourselves! The biggest lesson that I learned about the night that I got robbed was that it wasn't personal - I made it that way. Please remember that Life's not personal, it just feels that way sometimes.

Our perception is our reality whether it's true or not. We can't change the past but we can always change our perception of the present so that we can move forward to a more successful future. As long as we have breath, we will have negative emotions and experiences because it's human to do so but only when we challenge them, Do We Win!

SUCCESS IS IN THE EYE OF THE BEHOLDER

by Martha Cooper

After a wonderful career with the Air Force, during which she served in various management positions and received several awards, including the Outstanding Civil Service Award and two Exemplary Civil Service Awards, Martha Cooper started her next life adventure. Moving back to her hometown of Sacramento, CA, she joined son Alan in his painting and contracting business (Cooper Construction of CA) and established herself as an interior decorator, where she once again achieved success with her business Decor&You. She also is a writer and speaker, whose favorite subjects include Environmentally Friendly Design and Making Your Own Personal Happiness. She has been interviewed on ABC radio by Sandra Yancey, founder of eWomenNetwork. Widowed in 2002, Martha lives near her son Alan and daughter-in-law Graciela and her three amazing grandchildren, Gisel, Ivan and Yamil.

How do You Measure Success? I consider myself a very successful person. I've set goals for myself, met or exceeded them and moved on to the next goal. Working in both the private and the public sector, I've attained responsible positions and attendant compensation packages, with a six figure income that probably puts me in the top 5% of the U.S. population. While I'm proud of what I've achieved, especially as a woman in the business world, the accomplishments of someone who is very close to me far outweigh anything I've been able to attain.

My daughter-in-law Graciela is a hero to me and an example of success for many reasons. She came to the U.S. from Argentina with $300 in her pocket and three small children in tow. Gisel was eight years old; Ivan was five and Yamil was four. Graciela didn't speak the language; she came here with a determination that she would build a better life for her family. Her then husband had preceded them to the U.S. but had not yet found work. None of these "facts" deterred Graciela from her dream of achieving something greater for her family and herself.

She has shared with me that many of her friends and family had urged her to stay in Argentina with the life she knew. She was cautioned about the unknown, that she might be rejected and find herself and her children in even more difficult straits than the "devil she already knew." She didn't let any of that deter her; she may not have known it then but she was already successful.

Graciela has described her first experience in the U.S. as "I was in shock and felt so small, like being in the land of the giants after leaving Argentina and my parents and older brother for the first time and going to an unknown country with a different language. It was an adventure to start a new life with three little kids, two pieces of luggage and only $300 in my pocket."

After a short period of time in the U.S., Graciela went looking for work to help support her family. She applied at many places and was hired at Target. One of my favorite stories she tells is when a customer came to her asking where he could find the toiletries. She was a little confused as she was seeing "toilet trees" in her mind's eye. Panicked and embarrassed, wondering if this was a special tree that Americans had in their bathrooms, she was searching for the right answer when she was saved by a supervisor who came by at just the right time and sent the customer in the right direction. The supervisor took the time to explain the meaning and they had a good laugh. One of the things I admire the most about Graciela is her sense of humor and her thirst for knowledge!

That was 20 years ago and since then Graciela and her first husband divorced, she met my son, they married and I have been graced with a lovely daughter-in-law and three wonderful grandchildren. Today Graciela is a very successful insurance auditor for a national company. Regardless of what she was doing, she would still be a success.

Whenever I think of accomplishment, Graciela comes to the top of my mind. She exhibits all the behaviors displayed by successful people. She started with a dream, which she translated into a goal. She overcame tremendous obstacles to achieve her goal. She endured several roadblocks and setbacks to reaching her goal - but she was not deterred! If ever I'm discouraged in my path, I ponder Graciela's journey and I'm humbled and reminded that anything is possible with the right mindset and action.

Graciela's story is important because it is a standard against which we can measure our own determination and commitment to success. Success is not measured in monetary terms but rather against one's own purpose and goals.

When I might be tempted to give in or give up all I have to do in consider Graciela and how far she has come. I have been incredibly blessed to know this wonderful woman and to learn from her. She has helped me to learn gratitude for all I have and the things that I once might have taken for granted. Her success has added to my ability to attain my goals and to my success.

I titled this essay "Success is in the Eye of the Beholder" because I believe that success is a personal passage tied directly to individual goals. I hope that Graciela's story has inspired your journey as it has mine. Whatever your personal goals, I wish you success!

A SETBACK IS A SETUP FOR A COMEBACK

By Reverend Steven Craft

Reverend Steven Craft holds a M.Div from Harvard Divinity School and a B.A from Central Bible College.

He has served as a Prison Chaplain at various Correctional Facilities in Missouri, Louisiana, and Pennsylvania.

Reverend Craft is a Motivational Speaker and Author, speaking on the topics of Religion, Race, Crime Prevention, and Substance Abuse.

He is a Certified Facilitator for The Johnson Recovery Ambassador Institute and The National Fatherhood Institute.

CONTACT INFORMATION

Reverend Steven Louis Craft

P.O. Box 6183

Monroe Township, New Jersey 08831

Slcraft1@verizon.net

(732)682-2741-C

"Amazing Grace, how sweet the sound that saved a wretch like me; I once was lost but now I'm found; was blind, but now I see."

My own comeback from a former life of drug addiction and crime proves that positive change is indeed possible. These changes do not occur in a vacuum, because we are spiritual and moral beings who have the capacity to make sound moral choices in life.

Criminal behavior, at its root, is a spiritual and moral problem which proceeds from the condition of the criminal mindset and lifestyle. It is the condition characterized by the lack of understanding of who we are in God's Creation.

Those who believe that human nature is basically good do fail to explain the things that we do that are definitely evil. A theological truth that explains this fact is found in the Gospel of Mark, chapter 7, verse 21-23. It states: *"For from within, out of the heart of men and women proceed evil thoughts, adulteries, fornications, murders, thefts, covetousness, wickedness, etc. all these evil things come from within and defile the person."* Not only the Bible, but any daily newscast provides evidence that we are capable of terrible and violent actions.

Therefore if we desire to see a decrease in crime, we must change the way we think about criminals, and the way criminals think of themselves in relation to their anti-social behaviors. Punishment alone will not change one from criminal behavior. However, a change of attitude and thinking can be accomplished through spiritual and moral regeneration. As a former heroin addict, I committed crimes in order to support my addiction, and felt no threat of apprehension or punishment would deter me from my evil designs! This is why it is necessary to incarcerate offenders in order to keep them off the streets preying on innocent and law-abiding citizens. However, rather than simply recycling criminals back into society at the end of their sentence we must work toward bringing them moral and spiritual transformation in order to effect permanent change.

The Setback Era

I was born October 10, 1943, in New Brunswick, New Jersey. Having lived during the height of the "Jim Crow" era was very challenging for Black Americans. Having to live in racial oppression as second class citizens caused most Blacks to hold tightly to their Christian Faith. It was the Bible that gave us hope in knowing that we were indeed Children of God, and equal with Whites as human beings. The Bible, not our bleak circumstances, kept us rooted and grounded during those difficult times in American history. Unfortunately, I came to embrace a lifestyle of hatred toward Whites, bitterness, anger and black militancy. This, in turn, led to a lifestyle of alcohol, drugs, crime and incarceration.

From 1964 to 1976, I was caught up in a vise-grip of substance abuse and committed burglaries, thefts, forgeries, and drug dealing in order to support my cravings for heroin on a daily basis. My "partner in crime" was my first cousin, who we called "Jimmy the Weasel", because of his ability to do "cat-burglaries." He was also an addict, who eventually died from a heroin overdose in New York City. During this "setback era" of my life, I was totally out of control, having gone through numerous incarcerations, yet finding myself totally powerless to overcome my addiction, by sheer willpower alone. I needed God in my life, but didn't realize it then. It was that experience that convinced me that permanent change could only take place through a supernatural intervention.

The Setup Era

Finally in 1977, I experienced a drug-induced psychosis on Venice Beach, California and was hospitalized in a state mental hospital for a few days. It was that frightening experience that totally convinced me of my need for divine help and I recognized that only a Higher Power, much greater than myself, could restore my mind to sanity! At that revelation, I prayed, turned my life and my will over to God and let Him take full control. Christ gave me the spiritual strength, courage and grace to meet my personal weaknesses and I began to accept full responsibility for my criminal behavior. After the hospital released me, I joined a Pentecostal Charismatic Church and began to grow spiritually and morally. I did not return to my old ways of responding to problems, by resorting to alcohol and drugs, but instead applied daily self-discipline, restraint, personal responsibility, and Christian principles without ever returning again to substance abuse for temporary, yet counterfeit "peace"! I have now a powerful testimony of being totally drug-free, and clean and sober since 1977. By 1978, I found employment as a cab-driver and custodian and continued serving God in the local church. Eventually in June 1978 I married Edith Mae Austin and our first child was born a year later.

During the "setup era" of my life, I discovered that the same hope I received could be utilized by others struggling with life-controlling issues of various addictions. I was truly "free at last"! I was free from the bondage of addiction and being "setup" by my Creator for a much higher purpose in life! No longer was I being overcome with evil, but I was learning daily how to overcome evil with good.

The Comeback Era

I enrolled in Central Bible College in Springfield, Missouri in 1990 and graduated with a B.A in Pastoral Counseling in 1993. From there I was accepted into Harvard Divinity School in Cambridge, Massachusetts and graduated with a M.Div in 1996. I have worked as a Prison Chaplain at the Missouri State Penitentiary, Pine Prairie Correctional Center, and the Moshannon Valley Correctional Center. I have also worked as an Abstinence Educator, and Alcohol and Drug Counselor. My wife Edith works as a Special Education Teacher.

It is truly fulfilling to tell others, who may be struggling, that they too can go from the "pit to the palace" if they let God into their lives! I am a living example of the power of spiritual transformation having been free from addictions since 1978! I now travel throughout the world telling others the "Good News" through my Speaking and Writing Workshops.

In conclusion, let us rediscover the value of family, church, and morality, for with these strong foundations securely in place, we again will find true success, fulfillment, purpose, achievement and lasting hope.

For Further Information Contact

Reverend Steven Louis Craft

P.O. Box 6183

Monroe Township, New Jersey 08831

Slcraft1@verizon.net

www.christiancitizenshipministries.com

(732) 682-2741-Cell

SUCCESS IS A CHOICE – SO, HOW DO YOU CHOOSE?

by Laura Dominguez-Yon

Master Results Coach and veteran educator **Laura Domínguez-Yon** has an eclectic scope of experience both in the public and private sectors: editor, financial planner, insurance agent, credit interviewer, directory assistance operator, web editor, Personal Development Trainer, Laughter Yoga trainer, energy worker, and president of a non-profit. She exercises the ability to see humor in stressful situations and to highlight what can be gained instead of regrets. She prefers to be a part of the solution — not part of the problem, and wants to contribute positively to society. When she grows up, she wants to be tall.

For more information, contact Laura at www.LDYServices.com.

Is there something you know you should be doing, but just aren't doing? Like eating right or exercising regularly for improved health? Then, you see a story in the news about someone doing all the right things, but who gets a terminal disease or dies young. So you ask yourself, "Why do it? How will it make a difference?" Or perhaps you're developing a business and want to know the best way to market and promote yourself and your products but don't know what model to follow. It's a constant challenge to choose what to do and what not to do. For example, when my friend who lived in Korea for 6 years returned to the United States, she went to the store to buy milk. Simple! Twenty minutes later, she returned home without the milk, almost in tears from being overwhelmed. There were too many choices – whole milk, skim milk, low fat, 2%, vitamin enriched, acidophilus! The key word was "choice".

Every day we're bombarded with choices. Choice isn't black-and-white, this-or-that, right-or-wrong. It's multi-faceted – a wide variety of selections and more options than you can imagine. It can be overwhelming when you're working alone. Choosing correctly is very liberating and satisfying – the freedom of choice and the ability achieve and acquire what you desire. Having a guide on the side is essential for success – having someone to help protect your interests, who understands you, reminds you of your strengths and options, stimulates you to expand and fulfill your maximum potential.

Success is achieving and acquiring what you desire. Achieving success results from a series of choices. Deciding what success means, and what sort of success you desire is an important starting point. It can also be an obstacle. There are so many ideas and beliefs that confuse the choices for being successful. If you choose career success, does it mean sacrificing family? Or choosing financial success, does it mean jeopardizing your current social life? Do you fear "having it all" because it might be taken away, or you will become a victim or target of robbery or worse? Or does success mean showing the world all that you've acquired? Does size and number matter? Does it mean sharing what you have? The idea of success was an limiting issue for me: 80% of my definition of success was negative – target, dishonesty, manipulation, jealousy, greedy, selfishness, sabotage, failure, lonely. Was that what I wanted? No! Then I learned to shift my focus. Alone with my thoughts, I was too overwhelmed to address the fears and to focus on the benefits – influence, responsibility, choice. Instead of focusing on the problems, I learned to look at everything that was <u>not</u> the problem. Try this: Imagine a spot on the wall in front of you. Everything that is the problem is in that spot. Then shift your focus on everything that is <u>not</u> the problem – all 360 degrees surrounding you and above and below you. That spot is very small in comparison. There are so many more choices now in your awareness. I shifted focus from the problem to what is <u>not</u> the problem with the help of a mentor, my guide on the side – someone I trusted who had more experience in the areas of my development at that time: my coach.

The ability to shift focus is an important talent. There I was, at a low point in my life, in bed curled a ball and feeling that my glass of happiness wasn't just half full or half empty – it was a goblet, completely empty, tipped over, and cracked! What more could I do that I hadn't already done? My goblet couldn't hold anything at all! I felt as though I was looking through a camera lens at a movie close-up on that broken goblet. Then, suddenly, my view changed: the camera quickly zoomed out, away from the detail and expanded to the greater picture. There, beside and surrounding that broken goblet was a large banquet table heavy laden with abundance – and it was all for me! I became aware of greater choices than my former focus on one small detail of the whole banquet of abundance. I was awed to see what is available when I shifted my focus to what is <u>not</u> the problem. Later, like my friend buying milk, I soon felt overwhelmed – with gratitude for all that is available to me, and with confusion about what to choose. I needed another guide, mentor, coach.

Get a coach! All successful people have coaches. There are many kinds of coaches and mentors with many tools and techniques about what to do: Write out what Mark Victor Hanson calls *"Your Future Diary"*. Create your *Vision Boards*. Visualize. Meditate. Feel it in your bones. Create a business plan. List your talents, desires, experiences and see where they converge. Build your team. Prioritize. Follow Brian Tracy's advice to *"Put first things first"* and *"Eat the Frog"*. How will you choose? See a useful coach comparison checklist and resources at *http://www.ldyservices.com/comparison.htm*. Choose a coach with the perspective to guide you without making you into a clone of him or herself. Choose someone who listens to your hopes, dreams, fears, ambitions, and talents, someone who encourages you to grow to in the ways you need and want to grow, someone who can help you overcome obstacles and inspire you to new heights. Choose the coach and the tools that best meet your needs. Choose someone with whom you can work – someone you are willing to trust. Choose someone who matches your integrity, communication style, values. Choose someone with whom you can be open and honest, and from whom you are willing to receive guidance. Choose someone who has the training and experience for you to achieve your results: a Master Results Coach.

Within the pages of this book, friends, colleagues and acquaintances present their stories, challenges, techniques and suggestions for your personal success. It's a great starting place to learn about coaches. And plan on many different coaches during your life time. Famed cultural anthropologist Margaret Mead believed in consecutive monogamy because she believed it's unreasonable to expect two people to grow together at the same rate in the same direction. While she applied that to marriage, it can also apply to your general relationship with your coach, although you may have different coaches at the same time for different aspects of your life – like a fitness trainer and a marketing expert. As you change, your coaching needs change. Expect to grow beyond your coach and welcome the next one who can help you grow even greater.

**"We are like fruit on a tree —
if we aren't growing, we're rotting."**

THE ROUTE TO DISCOVERING MY PASSION

By Sharon K. Fisher

Sharon brings a wealth of experience and expertise to the world of financial literacy. As a 23-year corporate executive for a Fortune 100 company, she created and guided strategic cost savings and productivity enhancement projects. The Company awarded her its prestigious 2003 Role Model of the Year Award. Sharon earned her BS in Business Administration from Oakland University, attending only night classes. While she lives in Connecticut, her real estate holdings span three states. She speaks internationally, is a certified trainer with the Financial Educator's Council and the President of the Fortune 100's Toastmasters Chapter.

Contact Sharon at sharon@sharonfisherinternational.com

> "There are two great days in a person's life – the day we are born and the day we discover why."
> – William Barclay

After life tried hard to take me out with two failed marriages and two bouts of cancer before I was 44, you'd figure I would have succumbed and called it quits. But as I prepare for another anniversary of renewed health, I realize Life hasn't been a party, but I'm dancing while I'm here.

My most recent journey started with a book given to me by a treasured friend and doctor in Michigan. I couldn't put it down; in the back was a coupon for a FREE 3-day event promising to teach me to Master the Inner Game of the Mind. Intrigued, I searched the website for a nearby event. There was one only one hour away within the next 30 days. Now what? I really had no excuse to NOT go.

I remember some wise soul saying, the only way to predict the future is to create it. I didn't think I had a future. Nine years earlier I had been given a 50/50 chance to survive five years. But wait, I remember thinking, I'm way past that DEATHline... I mean DEADline... I mean limit. That was November, 2006.

That day I decided to start creating my future. It's also the day miracles (that's the only way to describe it) started to happen. For years I had been at the end of my rope, just tying a knot and hanging on. From that day forward, I have repeated to myself, it's not about where you are, but where you end up that really matters. I knew right then, there must be beneficial new knowledge or wisdom for me yet to acquire during this lifetime, otherwise why would I still be alive?

---

by Sharon K. Fisher
55

One seminar in 2009 introduced me to author, Janet Attwood. She described her book <u>The Passion Test</u>. Passion? I thought that was something everyone else had already figured out, just not me. I could only imagine how it would feel to discover, then truly live my passion. Why not take the test? Here was a way to help me discover more. This one had no wrong answers. I tried it on …teaching Financial Literacy to Youth. That is my new passion.

I asked why that focus? Looking at my life as a single Mom to an amazing daughter, everything I had done to educate her was in preparation of my creating the message of financial literacy for youth. I began with the importance of her controlling her finances at an early age. From her first allowance, to soliciting her help with chores around the house (without pay) so we could live in our dream home, to getting her first credit card, and instilling in her the critical lessons necessary to reach financial maturity. Oh yes, we did cut the grass ourselves, wash our cars, take our lunch to work, have a job after school and create innovative ways to strengthen our financial situation.

With college expenses looming, the scholarship search began in her sophomore year of high school. How better to teach budgeting than give her the month's expense money with the responsibility of making it last. With the benefit of savings, grants, scholarships and summer jobs, Nicole graduated with a degree in the medical field … debt-free. No student loans to repay and a credit score over 740. With her savings and as a graduation present to herself, she learned the amazing feeling of negotiating for and paying cash for her first new car. She had driven the used car purchased for her at age 15 and made it last through college. Her financial goals shifted to saving for her first home. She would occasionally call on me for advice about which credit card to apply for, or how to open an IRA with her bonus money. This was how the Universe was bringing me along the path, preparing me, as well as leading me to my passion.

Taking the advice of Janet Attwood who said, "Always choose in favor of your passion", I sadly chose to leave a conference in September, 2009 in Calgary early and return to New York to attend an event being presented by my idol and financial celebrity, Suze Orman.

As I waited for the shuttle to the airport, I saw Marci Schimoff, author of <u>Happy For No Reason</u> approach the hotel entrance. "That must be her limo patiently awaiting her arrival. She spoke to me, complimenting my jacket! Did I hear her right? Join her in her limo to the airport? Me?" Like a small-town girl, I said, "No, but thank you, I'm waiting for the shuttle." My mind chatter flashed into overdrive. WHAT ARE YOU DOING? You have been to life changing camps, seminars and conferences. Haven't you learned ANYTHING? Pacing around my luggage, I reached deep inside and found my voice. "Can I change my mind and join you?" I heard from somewhere. "Sure, I'd love to have you." Those 10 seconds impacted my life forever.

Once settled in the limo, Marci asked my reactions to the "Engage Today" event we were both leaving with chagrin. She was on her way to an Awards Event in California … and me? To see Suze Orman in New York. I told Marci I was focused on following the newly found passion I had discovered by taking Janet's Passion Test only a few short months earlier. Marci grabbed her cell phone and dialed a number (even though it was a ghastly early hour of the morning). Who, but Janet Attwood answers. Marci asked me to tell Janet my "passion" story. She assured me the Passion Test gives you the means to align your life with what you most enjoy.

Those 15 minutes continue to guide me to take action and not question why someone or something crosses my path. I am grateful, say thank you and am Happy for No Reason, because I'm on my way to living my passion. Thank you, Janet and Marci.

by Sharon K. Fisher
57

"Clarity is critical to success. Clarity leads to power –
the power to act – which is the basis of achievement,
fulfillment and happiness in life. Without a clear
direction you are either paralyzed or running around in
circles. Worse, you can never reach your full potential,
because you dare not fully commit."
– T. Harv Eker.

Contact me through my website www.sharonfisherinternational.com to
hear more of my story and how I share the gifts of financial literacy. You'll
be glad you contacted me to educate yourself and others you love.

DESIGN YOUR DAY: OPTIMIZE YOUR TIME, ENERGY AND RESULTS!

By Nancy Hagan

Nancy Hagan works with business people who want to be **more productive, focus on their highest priorities and optimize their time, energy and results.**

A Certified Productivity Specialist with over 20 years business experience, she was not one of those people who was born organized. She studied with top experts to learn key principles to solve problems for herself and others.

Nancy is dedicated to *freeing you to do what you do best,* implementing **simple, yet powerful systems that quickly impact efficiency, productivity and profitability.**

Nancy Hagan

Organizing & Productivity Coach

Freeing You To Do What You Do Best™

www.EffectiveDay.com

D o you feel overwhelmed with the demands of the day? Are you at the mercy of whatever comes up, unable to find time to focus on the high priority work that would move your business and life forward? How can you create comfortable balance with all you have to do?

Reduce stress, improve productivity and increase peace of mind by *Designing Your Day.* "But, wait," you may be thinking. "I don't want to be boxed-in, rigid, in a straight-jacket!" No one does. The good news is you really can have the best of both worlds – freedom and control.

It's your own custom plan, including spontaneity and time for you! It will be much better than being scattered and overwhelmed, and easier than you think. You may have many of the components already in place.

Consider these ideas to simplify the process:

Set up a spreadsheet with thirty-minute increments that represents the time available during a week. (or print out the "Reality Check Time Grid" at www.EffectiveDay.com/realitycheck.php.)

Block out time for your essentials and customize with choices that are vital to your progress, such as:

- Thinking and planning
- Projects
- Meetings
- Phone calls
- Breaks

- Energizers (things you love to do that enhance your energy.)
- Processing mail & email
- Reading
- Commuting
- Relaxing
- Meals
- Sleep

Look at the most important things to be done each week. The 80-20 Rule says 80 percent of your results typically come from 20 percent of your activities. Take care to identify the critical 20 percent that will create the maximum impact. Ask yourself:

- What will move my business forward?
- What will move my life forward?

Group similar tasks and create "Designated Days". For example, project work, writing, phone calls, appointments, errands, etc. can each be grouped to get them done more efficiently while in that "mode." "Designated Days" let you *focus on what's really important for larger blocks of time.*

Decide the best place and time for each activity. Factors to consider:

Environment: If a quiet place that provides uninterrupted time is hard to come by, you may want to try one or more of these strategies:

- Put a sign on your door, indicating when you will be free. For example, "Available at 3 p.m." like professors' office hours.
- Use an empty conference room.
- Go to the library or coffee shop.
- Wear a special hat to let your team know you are focused on a high priority.

- Develop a workplace culture of honoring an hour or two of uninterrupted time. Watch everyone's productivity and morale improve!

Energy level:

- Do high priority and difficult tasks when at your best.
- Secondary and easy things, like phone calls and e-mail, later in the day when your energy is waning. Open mail near the end of the workday, but do deal with it! Today's unprocessed mail is tomorrow's pile!

Create "Windows of Opportunity" to help create balance. These modules should be blocks of time designated for focused attention. Start with 30, 60 or 90 minutes intervals. They make it easier to adjust how much time to spend on any particular task, help you remain realistic, and make it easier to say No! You can still be flexible. You are ultimately in charge of your life! Modules are moveable. Stay with your structure if possible, but be flexible to accomplish what you want.

Schedule blocks of time for your most important responsibilities— Focus Time, which means no e-mail, phone calls or interruptions. Just start, even if you don't feel ready. You'll find it gets easier each time, and gives you a real productivity boost! We don't find time. We must *make time*, or it won't happen.

Schedule only 50 percent of your day to allow for the unexpected, plus things often take longer than we think.

Designate a block of time to take care of "naggers"- those things that are nagging at you every time you see them ("Take care of me! You know you should!" etc.). Often they are little things, such as the pile of mail, or the phone call to correct a problem. Once you give them attention, they usually take less time than expected, yield wonderful relief and a sense of accomplishment, and won't nag you any more! Bigger things (such as a project) can be whittled away day by day. Spend 30 minutes, or an hour, for example, and then don't worry about it until the next time for it comes around. To *prevent* naggers from accumulating, use the two-minute rule. If it takes two minutes or less - just do it!

Eliminate everything that isn't vital to the vision of your life, and especially anything that conflicts with it. Is one more committee or surfing the 'net more important than the time you need to live the life you want? **Every day, include things you love to do; and every week, include things you want to do but never get around to!** Don't wait for "some day." Life happens now!

Adjusting Your Day

Once you have your patterns established, you will want to adjust for comfort and/or changing circumstances. You may want to keep a simple "Cue Card" of your basic plan for quick reference. List the days of the week and the main tasks for each day on a 3 x 5 card and keep it handy.

So what if things don't go according to plan? That's life, and that's the beauty of "Designated Days". We will never get everything done (sorry to burst that bubble). Wait until the "Designated Day" comes around next week, and do it then, unless it's truly urgent. But *Designing Your Days* makes those emergencies less frequent. Your mind can let go in the meantime, because you know the time is coming when it will get done. Or maybe you will realize it isn't how you want to spend your precious time.

You won't always adhere to your plan. Life happens. But you now have a framework to remind you where you want to be. Like the painted lanes on the highway, this framework will help keep you on track. Of course, you may decide to take the next exit for some good reason, or just because you need a break. But it will be a more conscious choice. You will want to continually evaluate and make adjustments. *Designing Your Day* will make your choices more apparent.

Final Touches

You may want to have little rituals to complete your day at the office: clearing your desk, checking tomorrow's schedule, removing cups, etc. Think of what you would like to accomplish, how you would like to feel, what would help you get there, and build them into your day.

Designing Your Day allows you to capitalize on you at your best, taking care of your needs and wants, and elevating your quality of life! Be kind to yourself. We are not machines! Abilities improve with experience.

Someone once said, "Time isn't money. Time is life!" Are you getting the most from yours by *Designing Your Day?*

THREE SECRETS TO QUICKLY BREAK THROUGH YOUR LIMITING BELIEFS AND ACHIEVE THE SUCCESS YOU WANT

By Terry Hickey

Terry Hickey, M.S., is a Professional Coach, Business Trainer and Consultant, a Certified Master Practitioner of Neuro-Linguistic Programming (NLP) and the co-owner of NLP Advantage Group. Through coaching, he focuses on his clients' strengths and resources, helping entrepreneurs and leaders use their energy to powerfully transform barriers and achieve extraordinary outcomes.

Terry's insight, experience and unique strategies enable him to guide people through processes that facilitate amazing change. With his assistance they abolish limiting beliefs that interfere with success and replace them with life-changing, empowering beliefs. As a result, Terry's clients thrive with new perspective, momentum and appreciation. (For more information visit www.terryhickey.com and www.businesssuccesscoaching.com.)

How often do you want something in your business or life, something you say is really important, but you can't motivate or even force yourself to make it happen? You're ready to step up in your business, maybe raise your fees, take action on your bold marketing plan or call higher-end clients. You even sense that more powerful, exciting future, but when it's time to act, you just can't bridge the gap.

This is how most clients walk through my door: feeling frustrated, discouraged and confused by their failure to take effective action on their dreams. Despite lots of determination and expertise in their field, they don't know what it takes to break through the limiting beliefs that hold them back.

After working more than 25 years with thousands of successful entrepreneurs, CEOs, athletes and coaches, I distilled the three most remarkable concepts to quickly break through blocks to success. These secrets help entrepreneurs gain the confidence they need to take action and finally say goodbye to self-criticism and doubt.

Secret One: "Just Do It" Doesn't Cut It (Except for the Few Times It Does)

It is common for high-powered entrepreneurs to think there's something wrong when they can't change their attitudes and beliefs on demand. Success gurus profess immediate transformation by merely adopting magic words such as "Just do it," "Change now," "Let go," etc. Such phrases epitomize the absolute truth that powerful beliefs lead to powerful actions. However, just *knowing* that powerful beliefs determine our actions doesn't immediately *make* it so. Every once in a while we experience a rapid change in beliefs, particularly after a major life event. But more often, limiting beliefs rule, especially when we really challenge them. You can have all the right business strategies, tips and plans and *still* get stuck when it comes to taking powerful action.

Why? Because it's not just about knowing the right things.

Creating the life and business of your dreams is an inside job. Beliefs and values determine your behavior, not the other way around. Without a clear idea of your personal money and success mindsets and beliefs—and the ability to shift them—, all your knowledge and strategies may fall flat.

When your "inner game," or success mindset, is aligned with your outer game, or the strategy of X, you'll be amazed at how easy it is to take actions that will allow success to flow into your life and business. For many people, the missing key is understanding *how* to let go of limiting beliefs and *how* to step into empowering beliefs that will make them soar. This brings me to the second secret, one of the most effective belief-changing strategies in my Belief Breakthrough Method.

Secret Two: Discover How Your Current Limiting Beliefs Have Served You

Limiting beliefs hold the key to greater self-appreciation and can fuel your personal success. Really.

This may sound easy to accept, but it is not.

Hard-driving entrepreneurs often feel embarrassed by beliefs such as, "I'm not the kind of person who can do X," or "I don't have the ability to make that kind of money," or "I'm not capable of doing that kind of work." Many of them consider limiting beliefs to be personal weaknesses that must be hidden or denied until overcome.

So what would happen if you acknowledged these unappealing beliefs? Ask yourself, "What have I been believing that has been limiting me?" Then ask, "When did I decide to believe that?" Notice how often these questions will lead you to an early decision, usually a childhood decision.

Childhood decisions about what to believe are made with the best information available to us at the time. Because of the narrow awareness and limited experience of children, these decisions lack useful foundations. Children adopt beliefs that aim to soothe uncomfortable feelings and create predictability and safety, such as "I'm responsible for keeping others happy," and "I must not be good enough." Such unrealistic beliefs help children cope but do not support adult ventures.

Consider one of my clients, a business owner struggling to raise her rates. Her inaction traced back to a childhood decision to help her chronically ill mother get better. At the time, she believed that she could prevent her mother from suffering further by not having or expressing her own wants and needs. Within two months of evaluating, updating and transforming her beliefs as part of several belief-change processes, she confidently asked for—and landed—three contracts at double her initial rates!

Unresolved beliefs prevent entrepreneurs from wholeheartedly following their dreams. Restrictive childhood beliefs operate in the background, often out of our awareness, like an old software program. Once limiting beliefs are in place, we tend to restrict our focus. We are only receptive to information and experiences that support our limiting beliefs, and we ignore information and experiences that might cause us to reconsider or release those beliefs.

Yet, like software, beliefs need to be updated. Your ability to appreciate and acknowledge the positive intent of early childhood beliefs allows you to uncover your personal mindset blocks—the emotional tripwires that keep you discounting and doubting yourself—and then eliminate them once and for all.

Isn't it interesting that while a certain belief made a great deal of sense at the time, getting what you want today will require a new belief to be in place?

Secret Three: Embody a Perspective That Creates Greater Possibility

As Einstein said, *"We can't solve problems by using the same kind of thinking we used when we created them,"* and *"Imagination is more important than knowledge."*

Initially, my clients often say, "I'm stuck, and something is in the way. If I could just get see this problem differently. If I could only get some distance and see things from a different perspective."

Here is one way to consistently create perspectives that allow limiting beliefs to change.

Stand up and think of a problem that has prevented you from moving forward in your business.

Now, step away from the problem in a way that will allow you to think differently about it. Physically move and see yourself and the problem "out there."

Now, imagine stepping into the future, into a time when you have already solved the problem. What would the future you tell the current you to do? What would be the very next step? How would the future you encourage today's you?

Notice how just taking a different perspective and imagining a solution can begin a shift from frustration to possibility.

Keep in mind that change requires both intent *and* action. It's like the old riddle, "There are six frogs on a lily pad and one of them decides to jump. How many frogs are on the lily pad?"

The answer is six because he just *decided*; he hasn't yet *jumped*.

In summary, your beliefs determine your behavior and therefore your success. So when you are stuck, trying to talk yourself into believing differently or focusing on gaining more information and experience may not get the results you want. Consider what specific beliefs are interfering in your progress and be willing to explore how those beliefs held value at one time in your life. Then move your body and step out of your limited perspective so you can experience a mindset and physiology that represents the larger, truer you. This future you then guides you towards success with unique encouragement and strategies tailored to you.

Remember that belief changes can occur with the help of a trusted mentor, through continued self-examination, or as a result of experiencing profound life events. Alternatively, you can seek out belief-change experts experienced in resolving limiting beliefs and holding powerful states of possibility.

Applying these three belief-changing secrets gives you the freedom, motivation and guidance needed to achieve the personal and professional success of your dreams.

Now that you realize the power of beliefs to expand your life and business, what is your next leap to action?

If you have any questions about this article or would like to contact me for more information, please visit www.terryhickey.com.

THE SECRET I WAS LUCKY ENOUGH TO LEARN IN TIME TO CHANGE MY LIFE

By Lorelei Kraft

Lorelei Kraft is an author, producer, speaker and coach. She was the Minnesota Woman Business Owner of The Year, and her entrepreneurial successes have been featured in numerous national and regional magazines. Her latest book is: "Anything Is Possible! What You Can Learn From A Little Country Girl Who Went From A Two-Room School To Building An Award-Winning Village In Just Five Weeks And Five Days." She also produced a highly acclaimed documentary, "Five Weeks And Five Days," of that "impossible" story. Lorelei lives in northern Minnesota, and you can find more information about her at www.loreleikraft.com.

I've gone through many setbacks over the years and I've watched other people go through setbacks as well. People seem to fall into two categories. The successful ones are the "Yes—I'm going to change that!" people who get up and do something about the circumstances in their lives that aren't working. And then there are the "Yes but..." people who refuse to change their focus to something positive and choose instead to remain stuck in their misery.

When I got divorced after 16 years of marriage, I noticed there were times I was miserable. Every time I washed clothes, I cried. When I went into the living room, I cried. When I listened to opera, I cried.

I realized that when I washed clothes the tears always came flooding when I picked up the box of Tide—because that's what I had used when I washed his clothes. I cried when I went into the living room because the chair he always sat in was empty and that was the first thing I saw when I came in from the kitchen. I cried listening to classical music because that was our favorite music as a couple.

However, the one thing I don't like is to not be happy. So I switched to washing clothes in Cheer instead of Tide. I rearranged the living room so his chair was in the corner I didn't see when I entered the room. I switched to country-western music (which is about as far as you can get from classical!)

I knew these changes didn't have to be permanent. It was just that right at that moment those things caused pain, and I didn't like feeling miserable. I knew when I recovered emotionally from the divorce I could go back to the way things had been—if I wanted to.

---

by Lorelei Kraft

Over the next months I started doing informal counseling with others going through divorces. There were those who said about things that caused them pain, "OK! I'm going to get rid of that for right now!" And then there were the "Yes but..." people. "But I've always washed with Tide!" "But I like the living room that way!" "But classical music is my favorite!" These people preferred wallowing in pain every day rather than temporarily getting rid of something that hurt.

To succeed in anything, you need to make sure that you are in the "Yes, I'll change that!" category and not the "Yes but..." one.

Years before my divorce, I was lucky enough to have read an Ann Landers column in which a reader asked where she got her wisdom in knowing when to tell people to let go of distressing situations in their lives. Here's the secret to success as Ann told it, and it was from this story I learned the joy that comes from making life easier by changing how you think about decisions that have to be made.

When I was in third grade, the teacher called all the children up to her desk. She had a stone crock, a glass milk bottle sitting in the middle of it, and a hammer. The teacher then picked up the hammer and smashed the milk bottle. It seemed like a million pieces of glass were floating in the milk. She then asked the children, "Who wants to help me put this back together?"

The children all cried out, "But you can't!"

The teacher said, "You're right. And as you go through life, you're going to come up against all kinds of situations where you simply can't put what happened back together again. And you'll have to decide: Do you waste your time on an impossible task, or do you turn and go in a direction of something that you can actually accomplish? Use that as your guideline in life, and your lives will be much simpler."

Our grandmothers said the same thing in a much shorter bit of wisdom: "Don't cry over spilled milk."

I'm not saying it's always easy to do. But realistically, doesn't it make sense? If you can't change what happened, change the way you think about what happened! I had exactly that kind of a choice to make when my candle factory burned to the ground at midnight one hot Minnesota evening in early August.

The next morning I stood surveying the smoking, smoldering ruins. I didn't cry one tear. Instead, I got on the phone and started calling suppliers. "I need more wax!" "I need more wicking as soon as you can get it here!" "How fast can you get me some more molds?"

There were people I think I actually offended because they wanted me to be crying and wringing my hands and weeping and wailing so they could commiserate with me. But if I had done that, all I would have accomplished would have been to waste my energy on something non-productive. Instead I put all that energy into rebuilding.

"Yes but..." people also often blame others for the circumstances of their life. (*I was a poor child; I came from a bad neighborhood; my father was an alcoholic, etc.*) Yet the people who succeed are those who, if they can't find the right conditions for success, simply create the ones they need instead of using poor circumstances as an excuse for not succeeding. I went to a two-room grade school in a poor rural town for the first eight years of my schooling, and there were only 12 in my high school graduating class. Some could see my having that limited education as an excuse for me to not to even attempt to venture out of my comfort zone. Yet I never let that stop me from creating award-winning businesses in areas in which I had no training—and having fun while I did it.

Your attitude cannot be to give up if you think you've failed because something doesn't turn out the way you wanted it to. Successful people always see supposed failure differently than "normal" people who just give up. When Thomas Edison was asked what it felt like because his first thousand times at making a light bulb were failures, he said, "We now know a thousand ways not to build a light bulb. Each one is a step forward."

Life has handed me a number of blows, and many things have not turned out the way I wanted. But I believe that all of life is a learning lesson. My life started getting infinitely better when I stopped crying out, "Why is this happening to me?"— started saying instead, "What am I supposed to be learning from this?"— and then looked for the proverbial silver lining in what had happened.

People stay in "Yes but...." ruts because they are afraid to make a decision that might send them in the wrong direction. So what? If you don't like where that direction ends up taking you, turn and go the other way. Life is a great adventure!

HOW TO CLOSE MORE BUSINESS

By Tommy Lee

Tommy Lee (born in Cornwall, NY) is a successful entrepreneur, business coach, author and speaker. His presentations and seminars have helped many small businesses increase their revenues, retain their clients and maximize their sales. Mr. Lee has been training in the martial arts for over 35 years and is the proud owner of two successful martial arts studios and a consulting company. During his extensive travels throughout the U.S. and abroad, Mr. Lee has helped others to be successful in addition to continuing to attend training to further enhance his own knowledge. Mr. Lee belongs to many Mastermind and Mentoring Groups that include some of the top names in business. Knowledge, dynamic speaking ability and an inate talent to motivate others has helped Mr. Lee in becoming one of the industry's top speakers and business coaches.

Tommy Lee

443-871-2724

www.PowerTeamCoach.com

Tommy@PowerTeamCoach.com

As a whole, when the word "salesman" is uttered, the general population tends to think of the door to door encyclopedia salesman, a car salesman, or the telemarketer that calls to sell you a timeshare, regardless of your wants, needs or finances. Your parents are the last people you would think of as salesmen, when, in fact, they were the biggest salesmen you have ever met. They sold you on the importance of brushing your teeth, eating well, getting an education, and attending church. The sporting industry is selling entertainment. Politicians are trying to sell hope and change. But, the fact of the matter is that anyone who is attempting to influence another person to think like they do, or has a product that he or she believes can benefit someone else is a salesman.

If a business or profession is successful, then that business or professional knows that selling is one of the most important parts of the business. Whether you work for someone or you own your own business, in some way you will have to learn the art of selling.

In the business world, there are those who enjoy selling and those that do not. I tend to believe it is all in how you approach the world of sales. If you are only in the sales business to make a dollar and are attempting to sell to people that may not need your product or service, then there is the chance that you will not enjoy your job. If you feel that your product or service can benefit your customers, then selling the service or product is enjoyable and rewarding.

I have been in the Martial Arts field all my life, and have been blessed with being able to build a very successful business that helps people learn how to protect themselves, become fit, and gain confidence. Over the years, my company has seen many transformations. We have helped develop leaders and athletic champions. People who have trained with us have found that they were able to restore previous levels of fitness and good health. There may even be some lives that have been saved because of the safety and self defense techniques learned at my studio. None of this would have been possible if I had not been able to influence people into buying my service. Many of my students may never have experienced the benefits of martial arts. It is my honest belief that I would have done a great disservice to a potential student if I have been unable to get them involved in the world of martial arts.

If I lose a sale and the prospect does not become a member of my studio, there are three primary consequences.

1. The person may never have the opportunity to experience the many benefits that Martial Arts has to offer.

2. A customer would have been lost. Every time I fail to influence a prospect into becoming a member, my company will have one less customer than we could have had.

3. Every person that I am unsuccessful in selling on the benefits of Martial Arts is one more person that does not improve their health or fitness and one more person that may not be able to protect themselves against an attack.

This third consequence is the main reason why I work so hard at enrolling every potential student that walks through the doors. It is my responsibility to show everyone, regardless of age, the benefits of what Martial Arts can do for them. I owe it to them.

It is your responsibility and obligation to present your product or service to the best of your ability, so your potential client or customer makes a purchase. If you fail to sell your service or product, then you are not only doing a disservice to yourself and to your business, you are also doing a disservice to your potential client or customer as well.

The most important thing to remember is to educate your potential client or customer on what your product or service can do for them. If you educate your prospect, you will not need to sell anything.

Understanding the Jeffrey Gitomer quote "**Why People Buy** is a thousand times more important than **How do I Sell?**" will help you to master the art of selling. I can attribute much of my personal success to a statement made by Tony Robbins on his Personal Power tapes that came out 20 years ago, "People only do things for two reasons, the **desire to gain pleasure** or the **need to avoid pain.**"

When preparing your presentation for your product or service, your objective is to deliver it in a simple and well thought out format. Taking the time and effort to do this will greatly enhance your closing ratio. The following steps will help you in achieving this goal.

STEP ONE: Create Rapport

It is critical to get off to a good start by creating rapport with your prospect. Be friendly and sociable. Establish some common ground through easy "neighborly" conversation. Keep your body language in an open position by leaving your arms and legs uncrossed, smiling and nodding in the appropriate places. This helps you gain trust and confidence and lets your prospect know that you are there to help them. One of the most important factors in closing more sales is building trust. You want to be sure that your prospect sees you as trying to help them and not just trying to get a sale and close them.

STEP TWO: Ask Questions

The only way you are going to know the needs, wants, and desires of your potential customer is to ask the right questions. Their answers to your questions will tell you why they walked into your business, what they are looking for and how your product or service can help them. While questioning your customer, be genuinely interested in them. Look them in the eye and continually check your understanding of what they tell you.

Make every effort to build a relationship with them. Find out what they really want. Always be sure to actively listen.

STEP THREE: Create a Dynamic Presentation

When you are presenting your service or product, you must make it as real as possible for the potential customer. Communicate clearly. Show the person the benefits of your product/service and personalize it to fit their specific needs or desires. Engage their emotions by painting a realistic picture of how and what your product will do for them and exactly why they need your product/service.

STEP FOUR: Overcoming Objections

This is often the most feared step for many salespeople. Keep in mind that the objective of your meeting with the potential customer should be to illustrate a win/win situation rather than a win/lose situation. By you selling and the customer buying, everyone wins. After determining the customers want, need, pain - the "why" of their meeting with you - and you have successfully conveyed the benefits of your service or product, it is time to help your customer move past any hesitation they may have in finalizing their decision to buy. This is the objection phase of the sales cycle. An easy way to prepare for the objection phase is to write down a list of all possible objections you may hear such as, finances, competition, quality, service after the sale, cold feet, talk to spouse, or budget concerns. Memorize your responses to these objections and be sure that your non-verbal communication matches your words. If you just speak the words without conveying sincerity you will lose the prospect. Role playing with other colleagues will help you memorize your response and make it smooth. There should be no objection that you cannot answer automatically and instantly.

STEP FIVE: Trial Closing and Sale

Knowing when to close a sale is one of the most important aspects in finalizing any sale. When you feel as though all of your customers objections have been satisfactorily answered and you have clearly shown that your product or service fits the clients needs, it is time for a "trial" close. We call this a trial close because it is not uncommon for the customer to still have some reservations that you have not yet uncovered. If you get resistance to the close, simply go back to Step Number Four and handle their additional objections. When all the objections are resolved, ask again for the sale.

Selling is simply the art of connecting the needs of the customer to the benefits of your product or service. Your ability to create the association between between the pleasure of using your product or service versus the pain of NOT using your product or service is essential. If you truly believe your business provides these fundamental needs, the sale itself will be simple enough to complete but it still requires you to develop your skills and establish a sales plan. *Create rapport* with your client, *ask questions* to get to know their wants and needs, *create a dynamic presentation* that lets them visualize what your product or service will do for them, help them *overcome their own objections and simply close the sale.*

HOW TO SUCCESSFULLY GET YOUR STUDENT ADMITTED TO COLLEGE AND GET IT PAID FOR WITHOUT SACRIFICING YOUR RETIREMENT OR BORROWING A TON OF MONEY

by Mark Maiewski

Mark Maiewski, Virginia's Leading College Planning Authority, is author of the book <u>31 Secrets Of Paying For College That I Guarantee No One Has Shared With You</u>.

He is also a certified college planning specialist whose unique real-world strategies and step by step programs have guided students into acceptance at their top-choice schools. In addition, he has developed a proprietary cash flow system that enables parents to pay for college without mortgaging their financial future or going into deep debt. Go to www.collegeplanningvirginia.com and download 3 FREE gifts to successfully jump start the process now.

If you haven't given a lot of thought to this oncoming train, you better. And you shouldn't wait until your son or daughter – is well into high school to do so.

College doesn't have to be a dream for American students, even though this is one of the most complicated, tedious, and confusing processes one will have to endure. Even worse than doing a tax return! **Avoid doing this process right means you have decided to pay retail**. You may not be able to afford that route.

The big issue, however, is whether your student will gain admission, since there are more students going to college than ever before. Competition for spots is fierce. States are cutting their funding and tuition costs are rising at alarming rates. Which means you the parent will have to pay more and your student has less chance of being accepted. College admissions now is becoming more complicated, because most parents have to **figure this out on their own** during what will be an AGONIZING, PAINSTAKING, and TIME-SUCKING process.

Let's now talk about the odds being stacked against your student. 27% of freshmen don't return. 33% will transfer during their time in college. 47% dropout completely without finishing their degree. AND the average student at a state college is taking **5.8 years to graduate!** How many of you have planned to put your student on the 6 year plan when you only had enough money for 4? What kind of hit will your retirement take with tens of thousands of dollars in loans to pay back as well?

Another huge challenge for parents is mom and dad procrastinating in the planning process without the right knowledge they need to make smart decisions for their student and their finances. Most parents are worrying more about where they are going on vacation or which laptop they are going to buy, than they are about paying for college.

Want some good news? One of the greatest myths of the process of obtaining a college degree is that students and/or their parents have to practically go broke in order to realize that goal.

There are all sorts of financial aid packages available to worthy students – government aid, federal programs, scholarships, grants, etc. These financial aid options aren't just limited to small schools or unpopular programs, either – they can help students attend the colleges and universities where they want to learn, and to study the programs that will lead to steady, well-paying careers.

So how does your student and you avail themselves of these programs?

You need to start taking the time to fully understand the process, which is going to require extensive reading, studying the admissions game and the positioning of their student. It will require knowledge of the financial aid system, how it works and whether the family will qualify for any money. It will require major decisions on who will take on this burden financially and how it affects their long term plan. Without this effort, you will most likely be overpaying for college, and the sad part is, you won't even know it.

It's such a challenging routine that many students and parents give up – which is the wrong thing to do. Want to make it easy on you? If you're not going to do the research yourself, then seek assistance from someone who can walk you through each one of these land mines.

A college planning professional knows the in and out strategies, because it's what they do on a daily basis. They craft plans tailored to individual students and families, helping each one reach his or her educational objectives while making it affordable for everyone.

Whether you're setting your sights on a two- or four-year course of study, a trade school, community college or graduate school, you can benefit from the resourcefulness of professionals whose only objective is to help you reach yours.

The key to avoiding the most common mistakes is to start planning **NOW**, whether you do it yourself or use a professional service. Don't wait, don't incorrectly assume that all options will be possibilities, and don't sell your student short. In fact, wipe away all your preconceived notions about the admissions and financial aid application processes, because a clean slate will help you better maximize your opportunities to qualify for and receive aid.

Remember, this is a process that involves multiple parties, and your plan of attack may need to change from time to time. By making your student part of the planning and execution process, you'll be helping them get started on the right foot. Making them an active participant ensures that they understand the immense value of this joint parent-child endeavor, and better positions them to succeed in their studies.

Please don't seek assistance from your brother-in-law whose kids went to school 10 years ago, or your friend who didn't file financial aid forms and borrowed the maximum parent loan each year and will be paying for the next 15 years.

You want to eliminate the biggest mistakes parents make when guiding their student through admissions and then getting college paid for. Know why your student wants to attend college and why they have picked a particular school and program. **Your goal is to create a focused student who has one major, one college, is in out in four years, and then is off the family payroll.**

Then you can start to put a workable plan together to lower your out of pocket costs while fitting this into your long term plans. Remember, you don't get to borrow for or get financial aid for retirement.

Do you realize that after buying your house, paying for college will be the second biggest investment of your life? Now, with tens of thousands of dollars riding on this, do you really want to open yourself to making just one of these mistakes? Of course, you don't. Trust the experts.

The biggest gift you will receive is <u>the peace of mind</u> that comes with knowing that not only has all the paperwork been lifted from your shoulders well before the deadlines and it was completed accurately and on time, but your student was matched to their best choices and you paid the minimum out of pocket cost. That was the goal, wasn't it? Oh, it also helps to know you still have a retirement account too. Congratulations, Mom and Dad, you should be proud for starting now!

BEYOND
TRAGEDY

by Augusta Massey

Augusta Massey is an attorney who currently lives with her husband in Las Vegas, Nevada. She is the author of two upcoming books: **Stay Fired Up, 24/7!** a guide to jumpstart your life and open the doors to success (copies are available at www.stayfiredup247.com); and the highly-anticipated **The African American Legal Guide: Finding, Staying, and Surviving Law School,** a compilation of interviews designed to motivate the aspiring law student. Augusta's passions include volunteering for children programs and empowering others through public speaking. To schedule a speaking engagement, contact Augusta at aamassey@yahoo.com.

The conversation always starts the same way. Soon after I disclose that my family lives in Memphis while I reside in Las Vegas they ask, "So your parents live in Memphis?"

"No" I reply. "It's just Mom and siblings."

"What about your father?" curious minds inquire.

"He died a long time ago."

Usually, that ends the conversation. But the real journalists go further.

"How did he die?"

"He was murdered."

Silence! Followed by, "I am sorry to hear that."

Me too, I murmur, me too.

Sometimes, if I am feeling particularly *generous*, I share the story that led me from tragedy to success.

Nigeria— December 8, 1996.

According to Roman Catholicism, December 8 is the Feast of the Immaculate Conception, a Holy Day of Obligation to celebrate the Virgin Mary conceived without sin. But the sin committed against my family on this day has been etched in my heart forever. The day began like any other Sunday. Mom had cooked breakfast. We had done our chores and then went to church late, as was our habit. After a long service and celebration at the Catholic Church, my family of eight had a long line up of activities.

I went home tired and eager to change out of my Sunday clothes. Dad paid a lunch time visit to a family friend, while Mom went to the library to study for her semester exams at the University. I stayed home, happy to be exempted from the flurry of activities, unaware that by nightfall I would almost be orphaned.

In the preceding months, we had been repeatedly attacked by mysterious armed men. In our last encounter, my older sister was bound, but she still managed to hop to the door to get help. Before she could get far, one of the armed men caught up with her. Enraged, he threw her down on the living room floor and swinging his machete, made ready to deliver a cutting blow. Instinctively, Mom fell on her daughter shielding her from the glare of the machete. Dad used his hand to intercept the blow, protecting his wife and child. Like a bad horror film, the machete connected with Dad's right hand and cut deep. He wore a sling after that. As a result of these incessant attacks, we developed a quasi-security system: bolting, padlocking, and fortifying all doors, windows, and gates by nightfall.

About 8 p.m. on that fateful Sunday, Mom picked up Dad and headed home. She drove to the outer gate and waited while Dad got out of the passenger door to open the outer gate with his left hand. Usually, we would run out to welcome our parents, but not tonight. We had been given stern instructions to wait until they had approached the inner gate. I heard Dad fidgeting with the locks as his left hand was unaccustomed to such work. Mom noticed some men close by, but there was nothing overtly suspicious about them. We lived close to a social hang-out spot so nothing looked out of the ordinary about a couple of men standing on the corner. Still she was cautious. Dad finally opened the outer gate and Mom drove in to park under the shed. We were at the inner gate ready to welcome our parents. Then it began.

The men at the corner followed Dad into the compound as he struggled frantically to fasten the locks on the outer gate. "What do you want?" Dad yelled at them. "You have taken everything already. Leave my family alone." Mom heard the commotion, switched off the ignition and turned her head to see what was going on, only to stare at the muzzle of a gun. A voice close-by said, "Move and you are dead!"

Due to the ruckus, we shut the inner gate, barring entry to the assailants and our parents as well. My older sister went to the power box and turned off all the lights. I went to check up on our nine-month-old sister sleeping in the bedroom facing the outer gate. We had to get her out of that bedroom in case the attackers decided to give our house an ammunition bath. In the darkness, we plastered our faces to the windows, trying to get a closer look at what was going on outside. Helplessly, we watched as our parents wrestled against fate.

Dad backed out of the compound and moved to the main street, leading the intruders away from our house. He was still screaming at them to leave us alone when they shot him in the stomach. As the first shot rang out, the man with the gun pointed at Mom's head became distracted. Sprinting out the passenger door with super human strength, Mom ran for the back of the house. Since we turned off all the lights both inside and outside, she ran into one of the ropes used for hanging our clothes. It catapulted her several feet into the air and she landed hard on her back. Jumping up like a cat, she leaped over the back wall, scratching herself badly on the fence lined with the jutted ends of broken bottles. Her sole purpose was to get to the neighbor's house and call for help. She barely felt the blood oozing down her legs.

On the main street, the second and third shots lodged two bullets in Dad's chest. Dad, in his flowing white attire and hand-made sandals, dropped to the ground on one knee. "They've killed me!" he screamed. "Father, they've killed me."

Dad's death changed my life forever. In the following years, I had to make a choice: would I let Dad's untimely death define my life and reduce me to a depressed, scared little girl, or would I use his death as motivation to overcome depression and fear while helping others do the same? I chose the latter. Through the love of my family, I found the strength to move beyond tragedy. My journey has seen me graduate college with highest honors, excel in law school, win numerous awards and scholarships, and work with top law firms in America. Today, I assist people and companies through the most difficult moments in their lives while guiding them through the bankruptcy process. By providing expert legal advice to my clients, I help them move past their financial predicament to a fresh start.

Everyone has a past and some pasts are filled with traumatic experiences. However, it is what you do after such an experience that determines how successful you are in life. Success begins when you choose to stay fired up 24/7 about your life and not let the tragic experience define you.

5 KEY ELEMENTS TO ACHIEVING MAXIMUM SUCCESS

By Tracy M. McClelland, RN, MSN

Tracy M. McClelland, RN, MSN pursuing DBA from the University of California is the founder and owner of Tracy M. McClelland Enterprise, Inc. Nursing Success System and Ycarte Health Career Center. She has been called electrifying by audiences she has spoke for throughout the United States. An author, keynote speaker and consultant for nurses, she lives the life she teaches and strives to be the change she wants to see. She has been featured in Pulse Magazine, appeared on DC TV and is the author of the soon to be released best seller "Secrets to Achieving Maximum Success."

Tracy M. McClelland, RN, MSN

Tracy M. McClelland Enterprise, Inc.

Ycarte Health Career Center, Inc.

Nursing Success Systems

1214 North Peterson Ave Suite P

Douglas, GA 31533

Phone: 866-384-8680

Fax: 912-384-4390

E-mail: ycarte@windstream.net

www.nursingsuccesssystem.com

To achieve maximum success in your business, relationship, and personal life you must be hungry for success! It must be what you think, sleep and breathe every day. In order to have success on the level of Oprah Winfrey or Donald Trump you must visualize yourself achieving maximum success. If you interviewed the two of them you would discover that they have a lot of things in common although their business ventures are miles apart. As any successful person does, Oprah, Donald and millions of others, they all follow these 5 Key Elements to achieve the life they desire:

- Set goals daily
- Develop a plan for success
- Remain positive
- Persevere
- Share yourself

1 Setting Goals

"If you want to reach a goal, you must "see the reaching" in your own mind before you actually arrive at your goal."
– Zig Ziglar

Mr. Ziglar emphasizes in his training course on goal setting that to reach a goal you must set the goal and write it down, identify the objectives and place a date on it, list or identify the obstacles, the people, and the groups that you will need to work with. Devise a plan of action and spell out what you need to know and write it all down and ask yourself what's in it for me.

By far I would have to attribute my yearly successes as a nursing entrepreneur to constant renewal of my goals each day, week, month and year. You should be able to quantify the results of reaching your goal or else you may have missed some key elements along the way.

---

by Tracy McClelland, RN, MSN
103

As you are striving to achieve maximum success develop new goals that will take you a step higher and allow you to grow and increase mentally, physically, and financially. One of my mentors, T. Harv Eker says, "If you're not growing your dying." As a nursing entrepreneur the sky is my limit for obtaining all of the success I can sit down and set a goal to accomplish. The moment I became a nursing entrepreneur, my annual income capabilities instantly increased by 50,000. It has always been my dream to teach and host nursing seminars and to travel from city to city. Well now that dream has awakened me from a sleeping slumber and I am living my passion and loving every minute of it. I am leveraging every disappointment, heartache, and humiliation I have ever experienced in my struggle to become a nurse and turning my nursing abilities into cash.

2 Develop a Plan to Succeed

"All personal achievement starts in the mind of the individual. The first step is to know exactly what your problem, goal or desire is."
– W. Clement Stone

In order to get where you want to go in life you must have a clue about where you are. Whether you are planning for success in your business, relationship or in your personal life everyone must develop a plan to reach their goals. When our daughter was in high school it was our plan that she receive a basketball scholarship to college. While she was only in the 9th grade we realized that this was still going to be quite a hurdle since she wasn't a great student in the world of academia. She enjoyed going to school but her idea of fun was snickering at the little boys and hanging out with her friends. She was a great athlete and a mediocre student who required a lot of discipline to whip her into shape. By the 11th grade she had been offered many athletic scholarship opportunities and even had a home visit by the Head Coach from East Tennessee State University. They laid out their offer for a full ride to college all expenses paid…now the only draw back was that she would have to bring her grade average to 3.0. Her father and I looked at each other and thought "oh my goodness." We knew we had a battle in front of us.

The following week the three of us sat down at the kitchen table and we begin to write down our goals each of them individually. In order to master a plan you have to see the full picture; where you are and where it is you are trying to go. So we wrote down each of her classes and the grades for each exam that she would need. We reviewed the syllabus and each course expectation. We even visited each class instructor and informed them of our new project titled, "Get this Kid into College under Scholarship". I created signs to go over our entire house to remind everyone of our goals. The goals were broken down into steps that must be taken on a daily basis in order to reach our goals. At the end of the semester our daughter reached every goal. She could not believe that this process worked like magic for her. She did get into college and has recently completed 4 years of college basketball under scholarship. Yes!

3 Remain Positive No Matter What

Take the first step in faith. You don't have to see the whole staircase, just take the first step.
– Martin Luther King, Jr.

In pursing my goals to become a nursing entrepreneur there were many pitfalls along the way. A part of keeping the faith is remaining positive and having that confidence that everything will work out for the good. You have to decide what's important to you and go for it no matter what. Associate yourself with the people who are doing what you want to do, going where you want to go because they are only able to be accomplished because of remaining positive. One of the things that will help you stay positive is to stay focused. Focusing on your desires can bring energy and power to any task whether big or small. When I decided to share my vision of showing other nurses how to become their own CEO's, control their life and turn their dreams and fantasies into realities; that was a bold step for me. I believe that we are directly responsible for our successes and failures and that as nurses we can choose our annual income. Through the tough times of locating the essentials I needed to pull my business together I remained positive that if I released my desires into the universe, and moved forward with action I could achieve my wildest dreams. Because of this I am a powerful anchor in my profession and nurses all over the U.S. seek me to speak at their events and for my professional business strategies to help them start their own Health Career Training Centers.

4 Perseverance and Determination

"Desire is the key to motivation, but its determination and commitment to an unrelenting pursuit of your goal – a commitment to excellence – that will enable you to attain the success you seek."
– Mario Andretti

Push beyond your battle and your struggles to reach whatever goals you have set for yourself. It really isn't about how fast you get there but about the character you build along the way. To achieve maximum success in my personal life I ignored what people were chanting. "Women can't be successful business owners." I have successfully run a six-figure woman owned business for nearly a decade. You determine whether you want to shoot for the stars or float adrift the clouds. You are 100% responsible for achieving your maximum success.

5 Sharing Your Gifts, Talents and Fortune

*"It is better to be prepared for an opportunity and not
have one than have an opportunity and not be prepared."*
– Whitney Young

In my pursuit for happiness, love, and financial freedom; I have lived by life with the understanding that if I give unselfishly of myself, my time and energy that I can have anything I want in life. It's true. When you are involved in matters of the heart where others are in need and you come to the rescue, the sky really becomes your limit. You can pick your destiny because you are guaranteed to be a success at whatever you choose. Every time I extend myself and although it places me in an uncomfortable position the reward is huge. In order to achieve success and enjoy it to the maximum you will set a goal, write it down, and develop a plan to reach that goal, remain positive and persevere as you share your gifts and talents with others. It is my pleasure to share my 5 key elements to success with you, and remember you are in control of your career, relationship and life.

MASTERMIND YOUR WAY TO SUCCESS

By Sallie Meshell

With over 15 years in sales, Sallie eventually started her own business – growing it to over $1 million in volume. She recently sold it to become a Business Coach and Success Speaker where she conducts training for corporations and non-profits across the country.

In April, 2010 her co-authored book, Direct Selling Power, was released which quickly became an industry best seller.

Informative and fun, Sallie helps clients create their own "Destiny By Design" - a blueprint for success to put you on the fast track leading to your goals, the bank, and beyond!

Sallie Meshell

Destiny By Design

318.670.7444

Sallie@DestinyByDesign.net

www.DestinyByDesign.net

> *"No two minds ever come together without thereby creating a third, invisible intangible force, which may be likened to a third mind."*
>
> *— Napoleon Hill*

Have you ever heard the saying, "two heads are better than one?" In theory, this can be considered a very basic form of a Mastermind group. While these groups have been around for years, they have gained in notoriety in the last decade with the growing popularity of Napoleon Hill's book, "Think and Grow Rich." This concept, as related by Hill, was inspired by Andrew Carnegie, the steel magnate. Hill tells us:

> "Mr. Carnegie's Master Mind group consisted of a staff of approximately fifty men, with whom he surrounded himself, for the DEFINITE PURPOSE of manufacturing and marketing steel. He attributed his entire fortune to the POWER he accumulated through this 'Master Mind.'"

The primary purpose of a Mastermind group is to help each other achieve their goals. Imagine meeting weekly with a group of four to six individuals whose sole purpose is to brainstorm, share resources and problem solve the current challenges you are facing each day. The power of your network comes alive through support, motivation and insight for each other.

Research tells us that we all have goals - whether we realize it or not. However, successful people, such as Bill Gates and Donald Trump, achieve more because they are very intentional and focused on their goals. Successful people understand the value of a Mastermind group. It is about multiplying their capabilities and knowledge by the capabilities and knowledge of the other members. We are reminded:

"Analyze the record of any man who has accumulated a great fortune, and many of those who have accumulated modest fortunes and you will find that they have either consciously, or unconsciously employed the 'Master Mind' principle."

As a self-motivated entrepreneur, it's hard to tow the line alone. We are limited to our own education, experiences and can easily be distracted and overwhelmed. Moreover, it's easy to stay in our comfort zone where we end up spending 80% of our time on non-important tasks. Many times, we spend our time "getting ready to get ready" instead of focusing on income producing activities. However, we can usually find success when we push through our fears and create new circumstances by stretching outside our comfort zone.

Mastermind groups are the perfect solution – it's like having your own personal Board of Directors. People join because they need access to knowledge and experience, but they flourish because of the peer group accountability. Accountability is one of the cornerstone principles of a Mastermind group as it allows your peers to hold your feet to the fire. This "public pressure" is a powerful motivator. The goal is to challenge you when the actions you take are not leading you toward your desired goal. Many times, we just don't realize we aren't taking the best steps to move us forward because we are too close to the project. The beauty of your peer group is that they are not emotionally attached and can therefore offer valuable perspective.

Through your new relationships, you will create a society of encouraging colleagues who will brainstorm together to leverage each other's brilliance and skills. They will propel you to raise the bar by challenging you (and each other) to create goals, implement action steps, suggest ideas and support each other all in an environment of total respect and honesty. Often, a colleague can show you an easier route that you didn't realize because of their personal life experiences or contacts. The group's experiences and wisdom create a synergy well beyond that of each individual.

Masterminds are one of the greatest "secrets" to success. Consider these benefits associated with Mastermind groups:

- Everyone is committed to success and achievement
- Diversity offers differing perspectives, input and feedback
- Teammates will bring resources and connections to the table you might not have had on your own
- Peers act as vehicles for growth by playing devil's advocate
- Great synergy is created with celebrations of consistent achievement
- Participant's brainstorm new possibilities
- Cumulative intelligence of the group comes together and is focused on solving your specific challenges
- Accountability structures are created to keep you focused and on track
- Draw on the experiences of other participants so you don't have to "reinvent the wheel"
- You have a shortened learning curve
- Everyone receives inspiration, motivation and encouragement
- No cost – only an investment of time
- Most importantly, you will see EXPONENTIAL results!

Furthermore, you will increase your intelligence. What? That's right - we are the average of the five people with which we spend the most time. Further explained, we tend to take on the habits, thoughts and attitudes of those we associate with the most. Therefore, if your Mastermind group is created of people at a higher level than you – you will automatically be changing your association and thus, your habits. Additionally, when you associate yourself with powerful alliances, you will be propelled to faster results. The key is to choose people who are already where you want to be. You want ambitious, open minded, goal-oriented people that will be mutually beneficial to the group.

While the concept of Mastermind groups was first introduced in the early 1900s, their popularity has grown as people, just like you, recognize the immeasurable power of brainstorming with others. They have evolved as a staple tool for the successful individual. Considered the "Zen for Business," they are now an essential part to any success plan. You'll gain tremendous insights which will not only improve your business, but also your personal life. Besides, the alternative is bleak – working alone is a slow moving process filled with obstacles and distractions. Stop the insanity!

Insanity: Doing the same thing over and over
and expecting different results.

Start your group – today! While a Mastermind group is one of the best success tools available to people, it is also the most under-utilized. Don't know of a Mastermind group you could join? Create your own – dare to be different. You'll have an instant and invaluable support system. Remember, to be in the upper echelon, you cannot be doing what everyone else is doing. Few people can achieve great things alone, but together we can help each other find great opportunity. Be bold – take action! Start today – and accelerate your success!

LEADERS PASS THE BATON IN THE RELAY OF LIFE

By Joyce Rice

Joyce Rice appeared on national NBC, ABC and CBS television programs, including *The Tonight Show with Jay Leno*, and lectured on The Art of Innovation for corporations such as General Dynamics and Rockwell International.

She speaks from her experiences and shares the proven techniques that developed her into "Best in the World". Joyce creates programs for all ages, using her unique talents to demonstrate how an Iowa farm girl became a successful innovator in entertainment and one of today's most unusual and outstanding speakers.

Joyce Rice is innovation in action, excelling in visual and verbal communication!

www.joycerice.com

888/453-9010

S he said to me, "You can't get in the high school band. They are good!" Her words hurt my feelings but didn't stop me from pursuing what most would view as unattainable goals.

It all began when I was ten years old and experienced an event that would drastically change my life. Until then I was a typical little girl growing up on a farm in rural southwest Iowa. The closest town was ten miles away with a population of two thousand. Like all rural children I attended a one-room country school. The big event was the PTA meeting, which was always exciting to me because following the business meeting there would be entertainment. The performer this particular night was a girl from town. She wore a white dress with a short skirt and white boots with tassels. As she was introduced, a march began to play. At that moment I saw a shiny silver stick in her hand that became a glistening blur as she moved it in circles, around, up and down, from hand to hand, so fast! She let go of it, but it kept spinning and then she caught it! I couldn't believe it. How could anyone do that? I thought to myself… this is so beautiful! If only I could do that! If I could just try! It became my dream.

One evening while visiting the neighbors, their oldest daughter showed me what she had gotten from the catalog. A baton! Nothing could have excited me more. It was beautiful, shiny silver steel with rubber ends and very long. She held the center and turned it so one end of the baton went on the inside of her arm and the other end went on the outside. All the children tried it, but I couldn't stop. I was still trying hours later when it was time to go home. My arm and shoulder felt weak, but it was my elbow that really hurt. It was red, swollen and turning black. The inside of my arm, my ribs and my leg were black and blue. I really wanted to twirl that baton; there was no limit to my desire!

Words cannot express my feelings when I got my own baton and went for my first lesson. The teacher was the girl I had seen perform at the PTA meeting. She was going to show me how to do what I wanted to do more than anything. I was so excited, but afraid at the same time. What if I couldn't do it? What if I couldn't remember? Before I went home I wrote down everything I had learned. Wrist twirl, right hand and left hand. Every day I practiced. Every two weeks I learned another twirl. Now I had the explanation to join my goal and motivation, which eliminated the frustration.

One day at country school my best friend asked me why I was practicing so much. I said, "So I can get good and get in the high school band." Then I heard her say, "You can't do that. They are good!" My heart dropped to my toes. My friend was two years older, she must know. That day seemed to last forever. As soon as I arrived home from school I got my baton to see if I could still twirl it. I could. I asked my mother if she thought I could get in the high school band if I practiced very hard. Without hesitation she said, "Of course." Then I told her what had happened at school. She said, "Don't let that bother you one bit!" and added a phrase I would hear many more times from my parents, "You do what **you** think is right and don't **worry** about what others say."

It was my first baton contest and my stomach started doing contortions, like I had never experienced. I knew I was going to vomit if I didn't faint first. I told my father I couldn't do it, that I was very sick and was going to vomit. I couldn't believe his lack of sympathy when he said, "If you have to vomit, you'd better get it done because they're getting ready to call your name." I said, "I can't twirl!" He replied," Sure you can. Go show them what you can do." He smiled and looked so confidently at his terrified daughter. Little did I realize the significance of my father's foresight. He was a quiet, shy man who understood my fright and was determined to help me beat it. I was thrilled to receive the second place trophy. Thanks to my father, I had learned to not allow fear to control me!

There wasn't money for more than an occasional lesson from a baton teacher in Des Moines and a week at a twirling camp in Indiana. Everything I learned I perfected and put in my routine, the routine I performed at the State Championship Contest. Since it was Iowa's first state competition and few contestants, I won first place, qualifying me to enter the National Baton Twirling Contest held at St. Paul, Minnesota.

Little did we know, compared to other twirlers throughout the U.S. and Canada, I was a mere beginner. The other contestants at the national competition varied in ability – from good to unbelievably great. It was plain to see I was far behind, but instead of feeling defeated I was inspired and motivated! I had seen excellence and knew that was where I wanted to be. I would practice twice as hard as all the other twirlers so I could catch them, the beginning of my Can Do Plan – Think it, Work it, Do it!

Two years later very good fortune came my way. The judge at the state competition saw that my routine was poorly constructed and asked if he could reconstruct my routine free of charge! This proved to be a miracle for me. He reconstructed my routine and taught me the "how to" of superior routine construction. The expertise he so generously shared made it possible for me and all my students to reach our full potentials. When I competed at the National for the second time I placed in the top twenty, the following year in the top ten. My fourth try, I **won** the National Baton Twirling Contest and was named "Best in the World!"

Who was I? I was simply a farm girl who wouldn't give up on her dream. I achieved my dream **and** learned that Determination, Discipline and Focus are vital to winning in any endeavor.

I am grateful to God and those who taught, inspired and supported me – all great leaders knowing **when** and **how** to lead. The help we need is usually very near. All that is required of us is being open to accepting and utilizing it. And, we must <u>never</u> give up on our dream. If we want it badly enough and are willing to work hard enough, it will become reality. Think It, Work It and never be afraid to Do It!

FAILURE CAN BE A SUCCESS!

by Darryl Ross

Darryl Ross is a graduate from James Madison University and began his career in the entertainment industry. As a lead singer and emcee, Ross was hired by the Department of Defense to perform in U.S.O. shows for the military. Ross and his troop "King's Six", performed in South Korea, Okinawa, and Japan.

From there, Ross was cast in the musicals "A Chorus Line" and "Sophisticated Ladies" and performed for Royal Caribbean and Cunard Cruise Lines. Finally, he worked in the casino circuit as a featured performer in Lake Tahoe, Atlantic City, and Las Vegas. Currently, Darryl Ross is a professional speaker, trainer, and consultant.

Darryl Ross

www.darrylrosslive.com

Do you ever wonder why things don't work out the way you want them to? You try everything you can but your new business, investments, diet, or even relationships fall flat. Have you ever considered that maybe... it was not a failure? Maybe it was a "stepping stone" to a much larger destiny. Without even knowing it, I experienced this first hand.

I was a professional entertainer for 20 years. Throughout my career, I was a featured singer and emcee for Royal Caribbean and Cunard Cruise Lines and was cast off Broadway in the musicals "A Chorus Line" and "Sophisticated Ladies." My goal was to be on Broadway! I knew I had the ability but just needed the right opportunity. Finally, the right opportunity showed up... I was called to audition for the Broadway Musical "My One and Only." The casting notice said they were looking for African American men, in their mid 20's, 6 foot 2, and athletic. Hello!!!!!! That's Me!!! I had never seen a casting notice that described me in such detail...I was so excited! The audition was at the Kennedy Center in Washington D.C. As I arrived at the audition, I noticed a line of people that wrapped around the block. I couldn't believe what I saw...standing in line were about four hundred 6 foot 2 African American athletic guys. At that moment, I realized that I was not as unique as I thought.

Nevertheless, I auditioned and did very well. I was asked to attend the final callback audition in New York City. It was my 1st time in New York and the audition went great! After the audition, the Producer of the show wanted to speak to me and 2 other guys. He said, "Congratulations, you 3 got the job! I want to hire the 3 of you for the part of the Rhythm Brothers. I'm going to Chicago tomorrow to cast some other parts of the musical and will have my assistant call you on Monday." I was elated! I walked down the theater district thinking, "I'm going to be on Broadway, I'm going to be on Broadway!" I pretty much told everyone that I knew…Mom, Dad, Brother, Sister, all my friends, and even complete strangers. I didn't care… I was going to be on Broadway!!!

Just like the Producer said, the phone call came on Monday morning. Without hesitation, the girl on the other end of the line said, "Mr. Ross, we're going in a different direction." I was so naïve. I had never heard that phrase before…I honestly didn't know what she meant. So I said, "what's wrong…are we doing the show off Broadway?" She said, "no Mr. Ross we're going in a different direction…we're not hiring you for this position." Click!

That was it. She hung up the phone with no explanation. I was silent. I was crushed. I was devastated. How could this happen? He said I was hired… he said congratulations! It was bad enough not getting the job but then I realized… I told all those people. I felt like a complete laughing stock!

A few days later, I received a phone call for a 1 day fill-in job for a show at Harrah's Hotel & Casino in Lake Tahoe. I was familiar with all the songs and was comfortable performing on short notice. I thought to myself:

Is this my consolation prize? Who wants a 1 day gig? After much thought, I figured I was available…so I flew to Nevada. I rehearsed all day with the other singers and performed that night in the show. I must admit, I had a great time but more importantly…I met a skinny little brunette dancer from Canada. Jennifer was a shining light to me and considering I was only there for 1 night…we made a very special connection. As I returned to my hotel, I thought to myself "now she was worth that 4000 mile flight." Today, I am very happy to say that Jennifer is my wife and mother of our 2 children. Thinking back, I was so lucky to have gone to Lake Tahoe. If I would have gotten that Broadway show, I would have never met Jennifer.

The next time you are striving for an opportunity that does not work out...
Pause! What did you experience? What did you learn? Who did you meet?
Your past was meant to teach you. Your present is meant to strengthen you.
But your future is meant to inspire you...to reach for the extraordinary in
you. Your journey was no accident...your failure just might be a success.

WISHERS, WASHERS AND WISHY-WASHY'S

There are only three kinds of people.
What kind of person are you? Or will you become?

By Enrique Ruiz

Enrique Ruiz's career spans nearly 30 years as well as many roles and industries, from manufacturing to program management. In his last role, he served as Deputy Program Manager on the billion-dollar 2010 Census for Lockheed Martin, managing nationwide Paper Data Capture Centers and Call Centers covering 1 million square feet of industrial space and a workforce of 15,000 strong. He has lived and worked in three countries. He is also an author, diversity trainer, inventor and speaker. For more information, go to _www.americasdiversityleader.com_

"The mass of men lead lives of quiet desperation."
–Henry David Thoreau

Oh, how we wish for the good things in life, the easy road, the fast track, optimum health, fun times and guardian angels to swoop in and lend support when things don't go our way. Even as children, we learn to wish for good luck and pray for timely blessings. How sweet it is to imagine our dreams coming true and to share those dreams with anyone who will listen.

And how disappointing and disheartening it is when those wishes fail to materialize. The work we aspire to do, the houses we dream of owning, the relationships we yearn for and the success we plan to boast are almost never achievable by simply hoping and praying.

These people are *Wishers*. They dream – which is certainly a prerequisite for success – but they do not know how to take action. They wish for the present to be better and/or that they had done something differently in the past. But they rarely create the futures they want because they don't employ the three P's (persistence, perspiration and passion) which would propel them to success.

Others eventually get frustrated with this ineffective strategy and take some action. But when the waters get rough (and they often will), many will abandon ship in search of a less bumpy ride. And in this floundering quest to find the path of least resistance, they achieve more than *Wishers* but still less than their potential. These people are *Wishy-Washy*.

Wishy-Washy's often appear successful to others, but by their own definitions of success, they fail more often than not. They pursue careers in one subject but, for some reason, work unhappily in other fields. Or they frequently change jobs, always seeking short cuts to greener pastures. They start out on paths that could get them to their goals, but they change course so often that they accomplish far less than they talk about it. Like rocking horses, *Wishy-Washy's* create a lot of motion, but they stay in the same place.

This is why most of us "lead lives of quiet desperation." As the seasons come and go, we regret the missed opportunities, the squelched energy, the forgotten passions and the realization that we could have *made* things happen … had we only *done* something, or had we only stuck with it.

Earl Nightingale, who authored more than 7,000 radio and television commentaries and two best-selling books, asserts that only 5 percent of the population achieves unusual levels of success. They are the doers, the movers and shakers, the ones who are clear about their purposes and set out to make a difference, no matter what challenges arise. These people are *Washers*.

As Leonardo da Vinci put it, "Water is the driving force of all of nature." Like water, *Washers*:

- *Wash* away problems,
- *Polish* their skills,
- *Forge* new roads of discovery and possibility,
- *Give* to those in need,
- *Carry* responsibility responsibly, and
- *Breed* new life and potential.

Washers may not always succeed on the first try – or the second or the seventieth – but they keep on keeping on until they reach their goals. They accept that failure is inevitable; it happens to the best of the best. Albert Einstein's teachers told his parents he would never amount to anything.

Michael Jordan was cut from his high school basketball team. Lucille Ball was dismissed from drama school with a note that read: "Wasting her time; she's too shy to put her best foot forward." Walt Disney was fired from a newspaper because he lacked imagination and had no original ideas. Michelangelo failed more than 200 times before producing the perfect sketch for the ceiling of the Sistine Chapel. Elvis Presley got a "C" in his high school music class. And in its first year, the Coca-Cola Company only sold 400 bottles of Coke.

But these *Washers* paid no attention to the negativity of others or even to any perceived limitations. Life equals risk; if you have never failed, you have never lived.

Intelligent risk offers opportunity for failure and opportunity for learning and growth; it represents the stepping stones for progress. The more times we try and fail, the closer we get to the realization of our dreams. When Thomas Edison was asked about his 10,000 unsuccessful attempts to develop a storage battery, he responded, "I have not failed; I've just found 10,000 ways that won't work."

Sure, the research, training and legwork to achieve your dreams can be grueling, but the rewards are oh so sweet. Muhammad Ali once stated, "I hated every minute of training, but I said, 'Don't quit. Suffer now and live the rest of your life as a champion.'"

Want to be a champion? Success can be hard, if not impossible, to define, because it means something different for each of us. However, there are several formulas posited by business thinkers to quantify the *potential* for achieving one's goals. Brian Tracy argues that human achievement is equal to innate attributes plus acquired attributes, times mental attitude. Denis Waitley and Tom Watson say success can be measured by doubling your failure rate. Paul Zane Pilzer says that wealth equals your personal resources multiplied by your application of technology.

All these formulas have merit, but things really get exciting when you synthesize their brilliance. Combine these theories with Nightingale's assertion that only 5 percent of us achieve extraordinary success and you get the following algebraic equation:

$$\text{Success Potential} = \frac{5\% \text{ who succeed}}{x} \left[\frac{[\text{Innate Attributes} + \text{Acquired Attributes}] \text{ Technology} \times \text{Mental Attitude} \times \text{People You Know}}{\frac{\text{Number of Tries} - \text{Number of Failures}}{\text{Number of Tries}}} \right]$$

Where:

Sp = **Success Potential:** number of people who will reap *my* benefits

IA = **Innate Attributes:** advantages I was born with, such as health, speed, dexterity and memory

AA = **Acquired Attributes:** skills I have learned, been trained in and polished – such as my technical education, degree or specialized experience

T = **Technology:** my proficiency and application of such things as text messaging, standardized manufacturing procedures, international standards, e-mail, high-speed Internet, social networking, computers or new equipment, or software

NT = **Number of Tries Before Success**

NF = **Number of Failures Experienced** (always expressed as NT or NT-1)

MA = **Mental Attitude** (factors range from –1 to +1)

P = **People:** those I know who can directly benefit from my product/service

So what is *your* success potential? (Use the calculator at _www.wisherwasher.com_ to do the math.) What is that intangible aggregate of your qualities, peculiarities and traits that set you apart from the 6-plus billion other people on planet Earth? Have you built a character that will help guide your actions and keep you on course towards the materialization of your destiny – even when life presents obstacles? Does your character provide the foundation that will set the stage for your success by energizing your soul, communicating your worth and making a difference in both your life and the lives of those around you? Do others see the same qualities in your character that you see, so that you can become a leader?

Only those who can see through the visible can achieve the impossible! Become a *Washer*.

See what others are saying and get the book Wisher, Washer, Wishy-Washy: How to Move from Just Existing to Personal Abundance! - which includes a personalized roadmap to chart your own success - at *www.wisherwasher.com*

REFLECTION

By Rick Thomas

Rick Thomas, EdD., is a leading authority on leadership, team and organizational success. Rick has been named Corporate University Best-In-Class 'Leader of the Year' and has presented keynote presentations and seminars to thousands of people internationally in Canada, the UK, the US and Saudi Arabia.

Rick is a coach and facilitator, and a partner in *inaya solutions* - a consulting firm whose intention is to work with individuals, teams and organizations to embrace their higher purpose.

Rick holds a doctorate with a focus on leadership and human resources strategy. Rick is a member of the Canadian Association of Public Speakers. Look for his upcoming book entitled, *The Effective Leader: 3 Keys to Achieving Results, Relationships and Renewal.*

You can reach Rick at info@rickthomasspeaks.com

"The aim of life is to live, and to live means to be aware—joyously, drunkenly, divinely aware."

–Henry Miller
(American Novelist & Painter, 1891 - 1980)

I was facilitating a leadership intensive (workshop) recently when one of the participants indicated that he had never spent time 'thinking' about himself to the extent that he had in the previous few hours. The session was a precursor to a journey of leadership development and consisted of some serious self-awareness. Others also agreed that they rarely had the opportunity to engage in mindful self-reflection. And this is certainly not an isolated incident. Most of us go through life jumping from one thing to another: one book to another; one job to another; one spouse to another – almost habitually – without taking the time to think about how the experience may impact our behaviour; shift our way of thinking; or transform our actions.

Reflection – that intangible process of purposefully mulling over, contemplating, deliberating and just plain thinking – is something that we seldom find time to engage in, yet which is key to our success, key to our very existence. We may move forward in life, or change incrementally, from simply experiencing or practicing, yet it is through reflection that we truly learn, develop and transform as individuals and as leaders. In this chapter, I will present two areas wherein reflection is vital: to gain self-awareness and to recognize how we present ourselves to the world – how we 'show up', and explore how these two areas influence our success.

Self-Awareness

Leaders who hire me to coach, or organizations that contract me to assist them to develop leadership development programs, often first ask me if I can identify the secret to effective and successful leadership. Without hesitating, I respond by saying "self-awareness". If we are not self aware – if we cannot or do not understand ourselves intimately (how we 'tick') – how then can we begin to lead others?

Reflection as a process to achieve self-awareness is a foreign concept to most people and a scary initiative for more than a few. Peeling back the proverbial 'layers of our (personal) onion' may leave us feeling vulnerable and open in ways which we are not accustomed. The journey to self awareness, however, will uncover unique strengths and gifts that we may not be acquainted with while, at the same time, reveal to us areas of potential growth and development. The journey is not meant to be an easy one; it is meant to be one that will force us not to simply *see* our reflection in the mirror, as it were; but a journey which will allow us to observe, to understand and to become familiar with the person who is looking back.

One way in which individuals can examine how they 'tick' may be to consider their personal *preferences*. Preferences allude to how we 'prefer' to behave depending on the context or situation. Depending on the theory or diagnostic tool (and there are many), we may experience preferences demonstrated along three continuum: extraversion/ introversion, which allows us to identify how we prefer to gain our energy or orient ourselves to the world; thinking/feeling, which allows us to recognize our preference for making decisions; and sensing/intuition, which allows us to understand how we prefer to process information. And while our own preferences are natural and easy for us to exhibit – acting as our 'home base' – we all can, and must, acknowledge and tap into all of them in order to be effective.

Awareness of our preferences impacts every single area of our lives: how we engage with others; how we communicate; how we handle conflict; how we lead others; how we deal with stress, and so on. Using our understanding of self in a broader context will allow us to better understand and appreciate others. Then, our ability to adapt and connect with them, in the moment and in any context, will enhance, thus increasing our ability to establish and nurture relationships. So, when a colleague of opposite preferences to mine enters the room, I am not quickly pulled into judgment. In fact, I use my self-awareness to begin to appreciate his or her unique, and most often, complimentary perspectives. Self-awareness – understanding what makes us 'tick' – begins with reflection.

Presence

A close colleague of mine, Maya, is an executive in a mid-sized consulting firm. When she walks into a room, be it in a social or professional context, she exudes confidence in all that she does: she speaks with articulated confidence; her physical posture displays confidence; and she manifests confidence in her outlook and attitude. She has *presence*. But it was not always like this for Maya. Not even two years ago, I would have seen her enter a room very quietly, quickly finding a seat and timidly waiting for the meeting or event to begin. The same person, but a different Maya!

Back then, Maya knew that I had gained some knowledge and awareness about 'presence' – how we 'show up' or present ourselves to the world – and she was very eager to learn more. As a first step, I challenged Maya to engage in some reflective practice.

Establishing true *presence* involves making the most of our language, emotions and body in a coherent, complementary fashion. Each and every time we open our mouths to speak, we have the power to influence context. Do we set a positive, nurturing context? Or, having chosen different words, do we set one that is threatening or disrespectful? Do the words that we use convey what we want to communicate in a way that is complementary with our emotions, or are they at odds? Does our physicality support this message, or is the message our body is sending out in conflict with our words and our emotions? Our physicality does not lie! Very rarely can we deliver a highly energetic, motivational speech, for example, if our body gestures are not in coherence with both the way we are feeling at the time and the words that we are using to convey the message.

Reflecting on these three attributes allows us to more critically observe our behaviour while providing us the opportunity to determine their impact on those with whom we interact. Further, knowing this will allow us to recreate the presence that we want to live *into* and manifest *outward*. Maya, she tells me, still reflects on how she 'shows up' and tries to observe, in real time, how her presence is impacting others. Regardless of our occupation or path in life, understanding how we 'show up' in the world begins with reflection.

The Impact on Success

Success is almost as elusive as happiness to define or explain, and it is personal. One person's idea of success may be the exact opposite of someone else's. However, what is not elusive or unique is the impact that both the awareness of self and the understanding of presence have on success, specifically on how we consciously make use of what we know about ourselves to establish and maintain significant, meaningful, and profitable relationships with others. While an improved sense of self is natural, the true outcome of this reflective practice will be successful, sustained relationships in work and in life.

LIVING YOUR DASH FOR SUCCESS IN LIFE

Dr. Tony Valencia

Dr. Tony Valencia, President and CEO, *Live Your Dash Productions, Inc.*, exemplifies his philosophy of "living every moment of every day as if you are leaving behind a legacy." As Co-founder and President of *The A.I.M. Academy* he teaches personal development and motivation to youth, having success also in reducing recidivism. His college athlete recruiting company, *Total Package Sports Recruiting,* promotes high school students for playing collegiate sports on scholarships. And, as a transitional speaker, Tony inspires students on the importance of being successful from high school to college for achieving success in life, while also speaking on disability awareness.

When a person dies, there are always two dates engraved on the tombstone, the birth date and the death date. What separates those two dates is a dash, a small, horizontal dividing line that represents your life – all the memories you created while you walked the earth: the good, the bad and the ugly. It represents all of those people who you influenced, either positively or negatively, together with all of your sins as well as your good deeds; the legacy you left behind; the footprint you left on society.

text from my 2009 commencement speech at ITT Tech

Too many people forget to dream. Maybe it's not that they *forget*, rather they *refuse* to dream. We all know what it's like to strive for a goal and not achieve it. But this is only worsened when, upon not reaching that goal we are told, "See, I knew you couldn't do it", or "I hate to say it, but...", or "What makes you different from everyone else that you think you can do something no one else has ever done before?" The list of "I told you so" statements is very long because there are so many people in this world who subconsciously do not want you to succeed. After all, if you succeed, it would just become obvious to them how their lives are so pitiful and aimless.

Our friends, family and loved ones mean well; they really do. It's just that so many of them are caught in the trap of "same place, same thing." The mere thought of doing something different is scary to most people. I know people who have been living in the same home for over 30 years, with the same furniture that was in that particular model home when they purchased it! To them, the very idea of doing something so radical as changing their lifestyle is so counter intuitive to the way they think that it has never even been an option.

by Dr. Tony Valencia

There are others I know who have worked in the same job with the same company for one or two decades, earning the same 3% annual raise, driving the same route to and from work every day; and, they are MISERABLE!! But, when asked why they don't get different jobs, do something they actually like, or go into business for themselves, they look at you as if you have three eyes! It's been said that most people will do just enough work as to not be fired, and most employers will pay people just enough money so they won't quit! Years ago a survey was taken by Time Magazine and it was discovered that our society is full of people not working – it's just good for them that they're still employed! Welcome to Corporate America! And, my family always wondered why I never worked in a "traditional job".

I have a 5 year-old-daughter who I just love to watch lose herself in her imagination. I could spend countless hours simply admiring how she names all her dolls and stuffed animals then creates fantasy scenarios of fun and adventure; and, how she never seems to run out of "ideas" for her "playmates." While growing up we all spent time like this dreaming. Unfortunately for many of us, growing up also meant growing out of our ability, or desire, to dream. And, even worse, we lost the courage to dance like no one's watching, to love like it counts, to sing like nothing else matters, and to live like we are invincible.

In high school we often felt that way, like we would live forever; like nothing's more important than what we're wearing today, how we look, if that blemish on our face is really noticeable, or if the boy/girl we have a crush on even knows we exist.

Tomorrow? What's that?

A career? Why should *I* start thinking about that now?

Save money? I don't need to do that because I can always just make more. Right?

Then reality hits. For some, it starts in college and when you leave home for the first time. I'm not talking about being a stay-at-home college student mooching off of your parents; rather, I'm referring to that time in your life when you take that leap of faith and move out on your own for the very first time. Remember how scary that was? There was a sense of freedom and excitement; and, yet, there was still a bit of fear as well.

Today, the statistics are that 25-50% of all freshman and sophomore college students don't even return to school. Why? Because they realize they're not prepared. Most high school students skate by without hardly studying (I know I did), and then are faced with the task of actually having to "learn!" For many, high school is 4 years of socializing, whereas college is 4-5 years of learning. But, if the foundation for success hadn't been laid while in high school, what are the chances of success in college?

If you've ever watched one of the all-time greatest movies, <u>Animal House</u>, you will recall a scene in the movie when several Delta fraternity brothers were in the dean's office. The students were being reprimanded for their lack of "involvement" with college standards, and the dean was reviewing their GPA's, "…zero point zero zero…" I've got to admit that my freshman year in college wasn't quite that bad; but after "earning" a 1.7 GPA cumulative for my first year, I felt like I could have been one of those Deltas!

My freshman year was <u>my</u> first year away from home, living in a coed dorm, and not having anyone telling me what to do, or what not to do for that matter. I spent so much time away from the classroom; instead, I was partying, drinking, chasing skirts and engaging in extra-curricular activities. During the summer between my freshman and sophomore years, I received a letter from the academic dean that read something like this:

"Congratulations on your less-than-stellar performance during your freshman year at our fine institution. Should you decide to return and actually get an education, understand you will do so under a new set of rules – ours not yours!

---

by Dr. Tony Valencia

You will be placed on academic probation and be enrolled in a course reserved especially for students with your academic prowess. In this course, you will learn how to read effectively, study properly, take tests, and actually pass your classes. Should you opt instead not to return, know that there will be no hard feelings, and we wish you only the very best at whatever you decide to do with your pitiful little life!"

That letter was the only reason my parents allowed me to return for my sophomore year, but only on "parental probation," too. Let's just say my subsequent years were much different, leading to my eventual doctoral degree and graduating fifth in my class.

Know this, what we did in our past determined who we are today; but what we do today will determine who we will become tomorrow. Don't let your decisions today ruin your chances for a successful future.

Remember, always live your dash!

"IT'S OK TO BE SPIRITUAL AND WEALTHY!"

by Deborah Wilson

Deborah Wilson is a contemporary spiritual teacher and healer who uses her intuitive abilities as an inspirational speaker, author and mentor of prosperous living. After having a life altering illness and subsequent profound encounter with angels, she was told that, "a better life was waiting for her." Deborah acted on the intuitive guidance given to heal her body and step into a new life and career. She works with the angelic realm bringing foundational spiritual wisdom as well as practical applications as a Radio Show Host, Angel Therapist* and Transformational Clairvoyant Coach helping people worldwide.

www.angelsandprosperity.com

It is your Divine birthright to create anything you want in your earthly life. You are the outer most directive expression of co-creative energy. YOU are here to play and grow and expand that energy. In a nutshell, YOU get to play out this life, YOUR life, anyway you want.

Even as a little girl I always knew that if I wanted something, I could make it happen. Children are very clear about their ability to co-create and manifest their ideas and desires into reality. Each of us did this with ease and grace until someone told us we couldn't. Then, for some us, life got a bit bumpy as we took on other people's beliefs rather than believing in our abilities and believing in ourselves.

Just for a moment, remember a time when you really wanted something to happen and you were able to bring it into your life. When you did this you were clear about what you wanted, you thought about it a lot and in your imagining you felt what it was like to have it. In other words, you were already experiencing it in the NOW. The feelings associated with this experience were good feelings bringing a sense of joy and well-being.

Now, remember a time when you worried about something happening that you didn't want and it happened anyway. Just like the positive experience, you were clear about what you didn't want, you thought about it a lot and in that same imagining you were feeling what it would be like if it were to happen. In other words you were experiencing it in the NOW. The feelings associated with it would be anxious ones bringing a sense of fear and anxiety.

Both of these scenarios exist because this field of co-creative energy is operating every second, of every minute, of every hour, every day, each week, each month, each year and it never ever takes a break or a holiday. It is delivering to you exactly what you are extending out energetically.

by Deborah Wilson

What this means for you is, that whether or not you are aware of it or believe in it, this co-creative energy is doing it's thing and you don't even have to think about it. However, when you are aware and when you allow yourself to become playful with this knowledge and your own power to create, you become as one of my clients expressed so perfectly, "Captain of your own ship."

One of my very favorite quotes comes from Michael Bernard Beckwith who says, *"You can't hide your secret thoughts because they show up as your life."* These thoughts are both conscious and unconscious beliefs that are directing your life. Both can be changed in any direction that you desire.

For me, positive change in my life happens by first asking spirit what I call "clarifying questions." I then "listen" for the answers and then I take what I call "guided action." I trust that my questions are always answered and it is up to me to be unattached as to what the answer is or how it shows up.

What I love about honoring my intuition and the spirit world is that I get what I call "insider information." At any moment I can access wisdom and information that allows me to be happier, healthier and wealthier in my personal life while also using this "insider information" to guide, inspire and show others to do the same.

One morning I was thinking about how so many people have beliefs about money, spirituality and relationships that are keeping them stuck, small and frustrated. So, I asked the angelic realm what I needed to know about these subjects. True to angelic form I received a perspective and definition larger than I expected:

"True Spiritual Wealth comes from knowing that your thoughts create your reality."

Spiritually Wealthy people understand this truth and are mindful of what they say, how they feel and what they do. They understand that whom they spend their time with and how they spend their time makes a difference. Should they get off course they more readily self correct their direction.

This information and initial awareness can be a bit shocking for most people at first. It takes courage to reconcile that ultimately we, each and every one of us, are responsible for how our lives play out.

The amazing and thrilling part comes once we awaken to this awareness, we can then consciously direct our co-creative energy in a focused manner and our life can become magical.

An example of this from my own life was when I was extremely ill. Within a 7-year period I was diagnosed and treated for cancer and an autoimmune disorder that turned out to be far more physically and emotionally life changing than the cancer had ever been. I was told that there was no cure and that the level of disease I was experiencing would stay the same or get worse. It was painful and debilitating.

Intuitively I knew that if my body "could get into this mess" then, my body "could also get out of this mess." I was clear that if I wanted my health and my life at that time to be different, than it was going to be up to me to make it happen. That knowledge and personal responsibility changed my life forever.

The changes took place over a period of several years. I shifted my diet, did transformational work, moved my family out of state, ended a 23-year-old relationship and changed careers. Positive change required more than just thinking positive, it required action that felt uncomfortable and sometimes terrifying. I did heal and the positive shifts rippled throughout my life.

If you play with even a little bit of this understanding you can quickly have a positive impact on your life. In fact, not only can each of us positively change our own life, we can directly affect those around us positively and serve the world.

We begin to experience a dramatic increase in synchronistic events or what many people call coincidences. I personally do not believe in coincidences because it implies randomness without cause and effect. This is in complete contrast to what was given to me by the very definition of "True Spiritual Wealth."

Everything that makes itself known in your life is there perfectly aligned and matching your co-creative energy. What we think and feel about what does show up, gifts us great opportunity to get curious and notice if we are happy with the results or not. If we are not happy with the results we can choose again and again and again.

Your life can then become what it was truly meant to be, an expression of what you want and desire as a direct result of your conscious co-creative energy.

This co-creative energy has many names. It has been called the Universe, Divine, Source, God, Allah, Quantum Field, Unconditional Love, Infinity and so on. Each religion, and group of individuals that allow a space for what they believe to be sacred, has name for this energy.

Guess what? I have some "insider information" for you. It doesn't matter what you call "IT." From the angelic perspective, "it matters not what you call us, just that you do." Meaning, we can label "IT" in as many creative ways, yet it does not change the truth, "IT" just is and always will be.

One way to look at it is like looking at gravity. You can call it by any name, you can believe in its existence or not, yet the truth remains the same "it just is." Having awareness and an appreciation of the Law of Gravity can and does have a direct affect on your life. Gravity, just like co-creative energy is doing its thing despite our beliefs about it or what we name it.

The more you open up your awareness to your "True Spiritual Wealth" the wealthier you become, not only from a spiritual standpoint, but also from a material one as well:

"True Material Wealth comes from feeling joyful about what you created."

From this angelic perspective we are invited to open up and go beyond our current collective and individual beliefs about what "Material Wealth" really means. Like anything in our lives it is the meaning, value and beliefs we place on something that makes it "positive or negative."

"Material" then becomes everything that you have and experience in your life, which has come into form from an alignment of your thoughts and your feelings. Regardless of what you "have", how you FEEL about what you have, becomes the true mechanism for measuring your material wealth.

This is not to say that you should feel joyful about something like cancer. What it is saying is that we can evaluate how truly wealthy we are based on our emotional state that corresponds to what is in our life.

I was not happy about having cancer. Nor was I joyful about the prognosis or effects of the autoimmune disease. What I could do and what I did, was to look at my life and take responsibility in how it was playing out.

I actually was so irritated at the doctor and his bleak opinion of how things were going to go for me that I got clear very quickly that I was going to prove him wrong. Getting well became a place of determination and excitement. See, it turned out he was the perfect doctor for me and for my healing. He guided me in a synchronistic way to heal myself.

I got curious and asked questions to that co-creative energy as to just how I was going to return to health. Then, I paid attention to everything and everyone that even hinted at being answers to those questions. As I paid attention to the ideas and inspirations that I attracted, I took action. I expected to heal and saw myself healed and I felt what it would be like to return to health.

Starting from where you are right now, you can easily evaluate from the angelic perspective how Spiritual and Wealthy you are. It doesn't matter what you have, it only matters how you feel about it and that you know you get to play YOUR life out anyway you choose.

Notes

Notes

Notes

Notes